THE STUDIO
AND THE ARTIST

THE STUDIO
AND THE ARTIST

FRANCIS KELLY

DAVID & CHARLES
NEWTON ABBOT LONDON
NORTH POMFRET (VT) VANCOUVER

0 7153 6499 5

Set in 11 on 13 pt Imprint and printed in
Great Britain by Ebenezer Baylis & Son Limited
The Trinity Press Worcester and London
for David & Charles (Holdings) Limited
South Devon House Newton Abbot Devon

Published in the United States of America
by David & Charles Inc North Pamfret
Vermont 05053 USA

Published in Canada by
Douglas David & Charles Limited
3645 McKechnie Drive West Vancouver BC

TO CHEDO
The Thousandth Man

CONTENTS

LIST OF ILLUSTRATIONS

PREFACE

Throughout history the artist has usually worked in the company of others and for a specific wage or commission. It is only in the last century that art has been created by large numbers of individual artists working independently without a previous contract of agreement and remuneration. The cycle of the artist working to produce pictures in quantity has come full circle in recent years with modern masters hiring assistants to help carry out their projects and commissions.

So little factual reference material exists about the lives of some painters in the early Middle Ages that they have been identified simply as 'The Master L' or 'The Master B', referring to an artist who is known to have worked in Louvain and another who worked in Bruges between approximate dates. Flemish painters of the fifteenth century are particularly difficult to document as few literary accounts concerning their lives were published in Flanders during that period. In the sixteenth century the diary of Albrecht Dürer provided an account of some of these artists. A few other texts contain most of the information we have, apart from their actual pictures.

One of the outstanding early books on the subject of medieval and Renaissance artists is Giorgio Vasari's *Vasari's Lives of the Artists*. The artists of the Renaissance who were contemporaries of Vasari are more accurately described than those artists of earlier times. In many instances Vasari had to rely on hearsay and supposition as well as an inventive imagination.

The wanton destruction of documents during wars over the centuries has deprived us of much priceless information. Although very little survives from which to glean a daily record of a specific medieval or Renaissance painter's workshop, we can build an impression of a typical workshop by

studying a passage from a document or an entry from a guild record. The
limitations of space have made impossible an adequate survey of artists'
workshops of many great cultures and sub-cultures such as that of Meso-
potamia—Assyria, Sumer and Babylon—which, to a lesser degree, challenged the art of Egypt. The Mediterranean civilisations of Mycenae and
Crete, whose Minoan city Knossos was revealed by Sir Arthur Evans, have
been omitted in favour of the greater glory of Greece. Similarly the fantastic civilisations of Latin America, Inca, Maya and Aztec, have had to be
excluded, as have those of Africa, Asia and Oceania.

The Studio and the Artist was prompted by the lack of a unified reference
on the studios and workshops of the past with contemporary comparisons.
I owe a debt of gratitude to W. G. Constable, whose book *The Painter's
Workshop* outlined medieval and Renaissance workshop practices and provided me with the initial stimulus for further research into this subject. I
have drawn information from many sources—books and periodicals, manuscripts, letters and contemporary mass media as well as my own personal
knowledge.

In making this investigation, my intention has been to convey some of
the functions of the studio as a workshop together with highlights of the
artist's working life as related to his fellow craftsmen and to the society in
which he lived. In the last chapters 10 and 11 I have included information
about the practical business of training and becoming a professional artist;
I hope that this will interest not only the artist and the connoisseur but the
general reader as well. Countless books have been written about artists and
the history of art. Many of these include recipes, formulas and techniques
of painting, while others describe and assess the artist's work and motivation. Few books deal with the practical matters of the artist's working conditions, his contractual agreements and the implements of his trade. It is
my hope that this book will add to the store of knowledge about the artist's
studio.

CHAPTER 1

PREHISTORY AND THE ANCIENT WORLD

CAVE PAINTING

Cave painters of the Old Stone Age established the earliest known form of religion by acknowledging the existence of unknown spirits that might aid them in their quest for food. We shall probably never know exactly why they painted and carved representations of familiar animals, with the occasional bird, hand, human figure, or mysterious diagram, but the artist's urge to paint may have been combined with man's superstitious nature and awe of the vast unknown to produce these amazing works. Prehistoric man probably believed that by drawing an animal on a stone wall, perhaps with religious or magical ceremony, he would ensure that the real animal would be slain during the hunt.

The cave artist possessed a remarkably retentive memory as well as intuitive artistic skill. He accurately reported fleeting moments, such as a deer poised for precipitous flight, listening in hesitation, or a charging bison, its weight distributed in relation to its forward thrust. Stylistically, our finest artists today would be taxed to equal many of these so-called primitive works. When one considers the elementary painting materials, to say nothing of the difficulties of working on rough cave walls in poor light, the feats of the first artists seem all the more extraordinary. The popular conception of man as little more than a hairy beast, groping about with a club, is shattered by the visual revelations of his artistic achievements.

Small slabs of stone with incised drawings have been found at the base of cave walls in a few regions. Some scholars have suggested that these were primarily sketches or even the work of pupils studying under a master in a cave studio. While this is possible, it is perhaps more likely that the stones were of greater significance in religious rites. The cave-as-a-studio theory is given credence since certain caves seem to have been used solely for painting over long periods while other caves were used as habitations. There is little evidence to support a theory of a sculptor's workshop among Stone Age man. The fact that many of the statues that have been found were of transportable size might indicate that their place of discovery was not where they originated. Therefore, unlike the paintings, we cannot establish any certain hypothesis about a central workshop for sculpture.

The earliest form of cave painting was created by applying pigments with the fingers before the artists learned how to fashion crude brushes. It probably derived from a still earlier form of decoration which interested man, that of adorning his body with patterns and designs. The drawings were produced by using the finger as a stylus to mark in soft clay or on decomposing areas of cave walls. These are often referred to as finger tracings.

At first drawings of animals were simply incised into the rock of the cave walls; later, having discovered colour pigments, the painters used black followed by red and finally polychromes in black, red, brown and yellow. The colours were ground from clay and rock using stones on stone slabs. When the colours had been reduced to powder form, they were made into a paste by binding them with bone marrow to which a substance, probably urine, had been added to fix the pigments. The hollow bone itself was then used like a paint tube to store the colours.

The paints used by palaeolithic man were obtained from natural earth ochres in varying shades from red through reddish brown, brown and bistre, to yellow. Black was obtained from manganese oxides, although black pigments from wood charcoal or from soot, such as that produced by burning animal bones or fat, were probably used, but these have not remained as well preserved as the manganese black. It is assumed that blue and green pigments were not known, but it is possible that some organic dyes may have been used which have faded with the passage of time.

Tools, such as stone picks and sharp flint burins, have been found in palaeolithic dwellings. The picks were used for shaping rock into bas-relief forms while the burins were used for incising outlines. These tools were fashioned by chipping and flaking the stone shapes under pressure. It was not until the neolithic period that man perfected new methods of tool-making by grinding and polishing.

All the cave artist's equipment came from his natural environment—the earth and the animals he killed during the hunt. Stone provided tools; the earth yielded colours; and animals produced the marrow for binding pigments and bristles for brushes to spread them. Both stones and flat bones were utilised as palettes. Even the artist's stone lamps were made of animal fat and a moss wick.

It is unlikely that anyone would suspect that stencilling and air-brush painting are among man's oldest art techniques, yet the caves in many areas of the world attest that they are. Early man used his own hand or that of a companion to create a decorative pattern. In the positive method of making a hand imprint on cave walls, he merely applied colours (mainly black or red) to his hand and pressed it against the stone. In the spray method, which is a negative form, the hand was placed against the wall, then colour was sprayed over and around it either through a hollow bone or a reed or directly from the mouth; when the hand was removed, an outline impression remained.

Cave walls, which were not prepared by laborious chiselling and scraping, presented the artist with problems of approach. Representations of animals were frequently painted over humps in the rock that resembled whole animals or sections of an animal. The artist incorporated the natural contours of the rock, with all its projections, ridges and hollows, into the painting. The results were pleasing and one can picture the artist contemplating the walls with a free-floating imagination in his attempt to discover an animal locked within its surface before bringing it to life with a few essential lines. The various groups of animals at Lascaux are so well composed that they must be the result of a studious plan to relate several juxtaposed compositions.

The constantly irregular surfaces on which the artist was obliged to paint demanded that he be continually inventive and not adapt slavish formulas. The difficult painting conditions which sometimes involved working high overhead in caves lit only by the flames of burning torches or small lamps, must have been comparable to those of Michelangelo's Herculean labours in executing the vaulted ceiling of the Sistine Chapel.

ANCIENT EGYPT

For 3,000 years the art of Egypt remained exceedingly disciplined, bound by rigid rules to which artists adhered strictly. Their style varied little in this span of time, and artists were quite content to emulate the traditions of the past with only periodic changes influenced by fashion. Their main responsibility was to suppress experimentation so that traditional designs could be kept alive in their purest form.

A complete village in which mainly artists resided has been uncovered at Deir el Medina in western Thebes. The village was divided into two sectors by a wide thoroughfare. The houses were built of limestone blocks and brick plastered with mud. They stood one storey high in groups adjoining each other. The interior plans were similar for each dwelling; there was a reception room, a living room, a bedroom, a kitchen and steps leading to a rooftop area where the families spent much of their leisure time.

For five generations artists lived and worked in hereditary employment, hewing and excavating tombs in the Valley of the Kings and at other necropolises. The artists worked an eight-hour day within a week based on ten days. This seems to refute the popular conception of slaves toiling under the lash while building great monuments, but it is unlikely that artists and craftsmen would have been subjected to such harsh treatment. Artists were often paid in kind with food and clothing, and some had servants to tend to their needs.

The community of artists achieved self-government and considerable independence. A village counsel was appointed which was overseen by the Vizier. Records that were kept in temple libraries were consulted whenever a dispute arose regarding the proper execution and style of a work. When complaints about the shortage of provisions went unheeded, the artists simply laid down their tools in what must have been history's earliest recorded strike.

Artists were generally regarded as artisans, very much as they were later in the Middle Ages. The Egyptian studios were attached to temples or under the jurisdiction of high officials, as were the cathedral workshops. Some scenes depicting artists show them working alongside goldsmiths, potters and woodworkers. Well-known painters were accorded additional privileges, such as taking part in the religious ceremonies at the temples, and several reached positions of high administrative or priestly rank.

The temple at Memphis of the god Ptah, who was believed to be the creator of the world and the patron of artists, smiths and metalworkers, was the principal art centre of the Old Kingdom. Painters and sculptors are thought to have been taught the precepts and techniques of their craft at Memphis and later at other religious sanctuaries. Apparently, the centre was comparable to a workshop of the Middle Ages, with a master in charge of assistants and apprentices. Disciples from the Memphite school went forth to other temples to influence and refine their style and technique. By the Middle Kingdom, with Thebes as the capital city, a number of studios were flourishing throughout the provinces of Egypt.

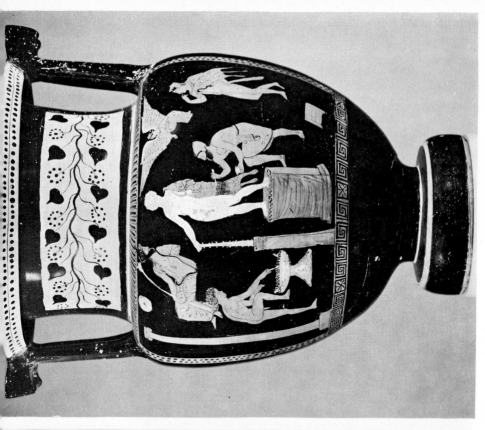

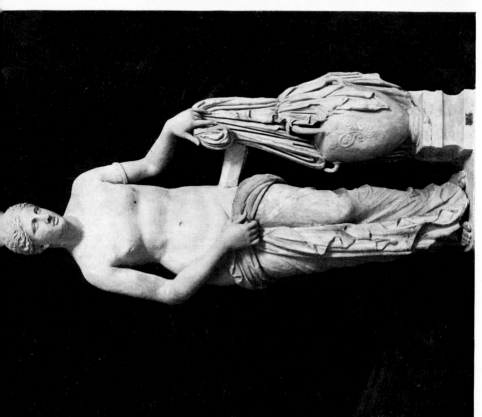

Page 17 (*left*) 'Venus' by Praxiteles, a Roman copy. (*right*) 'Artist Painting a Statue of Hercules', vase painting from southern Italy, fourth century BC, terracotta, height 20in.

Page 18 (left) 'The Thr
Graces', a wall-painti
from Pompeii inspired by
Hellenistic sculpture grou
this theme is said to ha
been used on signs f
brothels during the Renai
sance. *(below)* 'The Thr
Graces' by Raphael, paint
after 1515 when Rapha
was appointed Inspect
of Ancient Monuments a
Excavations in Rome a
Environs

Recorded titles, such as 'Superintendent of the Palace' and 'Master of the King's Works' indicate that certain individuals were singled out for pre-eminence in the temples or Egyptian courts. The highest post that a painter or a sculptor in ancient Egypt might hope to attain was that of artist-in-chief at the sanctuary of Ptah. Unfortunately, the attainment of this much sought after position was determined less by artistic capability than by heredity or influence—a situation which persists in some appointments to this day.

The daily work of the artists involved the decoration and maintenance of the necropolis tombs and various public works as well as making preparations for grandiose royal occasions. Superintending this work was a responsible task. The master had to have a working knowledge of most of the crafts under his charge. Moreover, it was he who decided the elements and style of the composition and saw to it that these were correctly interpreted by his assistants.

Sculptors held a more respected position than painters, as they had technical responsibilities requiring elements of the painter's technique in addition to their own. Egyptian sculptors carved mainly from blocks of granite or basalt, both hard to work but enduring materials.

Kings themselves indulged in the arts, as did high-ranking officials. Tuthmosis III designed a set of metal vessels as an offering for the temple at Karnak. In the sixth dynasty an important official like Mereruka depicted himself in tomb reliefs as an artist at an easel. Only a small number of works can be attributed to specific artists other than those created by kings or officials.

The style and methods used by Egyptian artists remained conventional and static for many centuries, yet the concept of tradition in Egyptian art was so strong that it assumed a role of virtue rather than that of a monotonous and repetitious process. Workshop regulations strictly governed a flat, stiff style and even prescribed in recipes the exact colours to be used on every object. Men were tinted brown and women yellow. Heads and legs were shown in profile, with the left leg usually advanced, while the shoulders were shown front view. Women were depicted with their feet standing together. The artists applied the tints of colour in a uniform fashion and handed their techniques down from generation to generation. This traditional representation manages to convey a sense of formal dignity and elegance of design which transcends time.

The art of ancient Egypt was primarily devoted to funerary purposes; life in the hereafter was the major preoccupation of the living. The most popular divinity and principal god of the dead was Osiris who was believed to die in the autumn and be reborn in the spring. An obsessive quest for immortality motivated the Egyptian's desire to take with him the finest possessions from this world on his journey to the next, in the form of scenes painted on the walls of his tomb, as well as actual objects.

The basic themes of most of the tomb paintings are the representations of the deceased's life in a series of generalised episodes incised on the stone walls in flat decoration without tone or light and shadow. Undoubtedly the painters often took liberties in extolling the virtues and omnipotence of the pharaohs in scenes of battle and the hunt. During the short reign of the boy-king Tutankhamen, the artists were pressed to invention in order to portray this slender youth's prowess as a great warrior and hunter.

Egyptian artists used six basic colours—black, white, red, blue, yellow and green—which could be mixed to provide other shades and tints. Red came from natural or burnt ochre earth or cinnebar; yellow was obtained from ochre or sulphate of arsenic; blue was produced by pulverising glass previously coloured with oxide of copper; green was derived from copper ore. Black was made from charcoal or charred animal bones, and white from gypsum. Gums and honey were used in mixing and binding the colours which were then formed into cakes.

The small, ruler-shaped scribes' palettes found in the tomb of Tutankhamen are thought to have been used by children, although the basic colours were similar in number and quality to those used by the professional artists of ancient Egypt. Slate palettes, often in the form of animals or fish, were used extensively in pre-dynastic times. These were used for mixing cosmetics to adorn the person with the traditional elaborate Egyptian make-up.

A few wall paintings which represent Egyptian artists at work indicate that small pots were used for holding fluid paint. Bags to hold the powdered pigments were made from animal skins similar to the bladders used by the old masters much later. Egyptian artists also used hollow reeds which contained colours much as our own metal tubes do today; brushes were made from reeds that had been pounded flat on the end to splay the fibres.

GREECE AND ROME

The outstanding sculptor of the golden age of Greek art was Phidias, who was active in the fifth century BC. His greatest works were the 'Zeus' at Olympia, and the 'Athena', which stood beside the Parthenon on the

Acropolis. The latter, more than forty feet high, could be seen from distant ships at sea standing in the sun against the blue Mediterranean sky. The chryselephantine statue of Zeus, thirty-five feet high and similar to the 'Athena', was constructed, as the term denotes, of an inner core of wood over which ivory, gold and bronze had been worked. Ivory represented flesh and gold was used for garments or accessories. Nearly all Greek statues were painted to heighten the sense of realism. Chryselephantine statues, which were immensely popular in ancient Greece, glittered splendidly in the pure Greek atmosphere, quite unlike the oxidised and encrusted statues in our modern cities.

Encaustic wax painting was a technique used to preserve and enrich the colours which were exposed to varied weather conditions. A number of painters specialised in this craft. The technique required the pigment to be mixed with hot beeswax. Surviving examples of encaustic painting are the well-known sarcophagus portraits from the Fayum district of Roman Egypt.

Phidias was appointed superintendent of artistic work at the Parthenon. While he was responsible for the concept in design used for the sculpture and decoration, only a small part of the many sculptures and reliefs could have been carved by his hand. He directed a group of sculptors which, judging by the quality of the work, must have included masters from Athens as well as other mainland and island workshops.

Many of the greatest works of Greek sculpture are unattributed, but a few, such as the late Hellenistic 'Laocoon' by Hagesandros and his sons Polydoros and Athanadoros, which is in the Vatican Museum, were signed. Sculptors are acknowledged to have collaborated with assistants on large-scale works; undoubtedly, the help of many slaves was needed to erect the finished sculpture. The size of some of the works might have made it necessary for the sculptors to work on or near the intended site of erection.

Pliny makes some interesting revelations about the size of statues. Particular reference is made to the 'Colossus of Rhodes', the sun-god Helios, one of the seven wonders of antiquity:

> The most marvellous of all, however, is the statue of the Sun at Rhodes, made by Chares of Lindos, a pupil of Lysippos . . . It was seventy cubits [102ft] in height, and after standing for fifty-six years was overthrown by an earthquake, but even as it lies on the ground it arouses wonder. Few men can clasp their arms about its thumb, its fingers are taller than most statues and wide caverns gape within its broken limbs, while inside can be seen huge fragments of rock, originally used as weights to steady it.

One cannot assume that all Greek sculptors were of legendary stature;

many worked at menial tasks of decoration. Fragments have been found which attest to the adequate but undistinguished skills of the average sculptor during this great age of art. That we possess any knowledge of the greatest masterpieces of Greek art is due primarily to the Roman conquest. Greek artists became the slaves of Roman masters for whom they made multitudinous copies of famous antique statues. These were consigned for export to Italy and other parts of the Roman Empire. Many of the copies have survived while most of the originals were completely lost or fragmented. The seven-foot statue of Hermes, an authenticated original by Praxiteles in the Olympia Museum, is believed to be one of the few surviving classical Greek sculptures.

Although Roman copies of Greek sculpture abound, only a few paintings have been found which can be traced as Roman copies after Greek originals. We must, therefore, rely on Pliny, Vitruvius, and other writers for much of our evidence as to the perfection of Greek paintings and painters. Some original Roman paintings have been preserved by the volcanic ash of Mount Vesuvius and a few undistinguished works are to be found elsewhere, but undoubtedly the best examples are not extant.

The artist's studio in the archaic period of Greek art was at first devoted primarily to sculpture, considered the most important of the arts. Painters later added the finishing touches to statues.

The first independent paintings were on small wooden panels. Easel and wall painting, probably in the fresco technique, were practised in the early pre-classical period.

The Greeks held competitions in painting just as they did in sport. Friendly rivalry in physical prowess and oratory were complemented by appreciation of the artistically gifted. Pliny describes such a painting competition held between Zeuxis and Parrhasios:

> Zeuxis exhibited a picture of some grapes, so true to nature that birds flew up to the wall of the stage. Parrhasios then displayed a picture of a linen curtain, realistic to such a degree that Zeuxis, elated by the verdict of the birds, cried out now at last his rival must draw the curtain and show his picture. On discovering his mistake he surrendered the prize to Parrhasios admitting candidly that he had deceived the birds, while Parrhasios had deluded himself, a painter. After this we learn that Zeuxis painted a boy carrying grapes, and when the birds flew down to settle on them, he was vexed with his own work, and came forward saying, with like frankness, 'I have painted the grapes better than the boy, for had I been perfectly successful with the latter, the birds must have been afraid.'

A competition of another sort was held in one Greek city with the entire population of young maidens disrobing in public to vie for the honour of being chosen as a model for an illustrious artist.

It seems that painting in the early days of ancient Greece was a family affair with father teaching son from one generation to another. We are given some insight into the early training of artists who were taught by masters in Pliny's account of Pamphilos, the master of Apelles about 367 BC:

> It was owing to his influence that first at Sikyon, and afterwards through-out Greece, drawing, or rather painting, on tablets of boxwood, was the earliest subject taught to freeborn boys, and that this art was accepted as the preliminary step towards a liberal education. It was at any rate had in such honour through all times that the freeborn, and later on persons of distinction practised it, while by a standing prohibition no slaves might ever acquire it, and this is why neither in painting nor in statuary are there any celebrated works by artists who had been slaves.

Pliny ascribes the transition in painting from the monotony of mono-chrome to the use of a wider colour range to the artist Ekphantos of Corinth in the seventh century BC. He refers in a passage to the colours used by the great painters:

> Four colours only, for the whites that of Melos, for the yellows sil of Attica, for the reds the sinopis of Pontus, for the blacks attramentum were used by Apelles, Aetion, Melanthios and Nikomachos in their immortal works; illustrious painters, a single one of whose pictures the wealth of a city could hardly suffice to buy.

Most Greek painting was based on polychromatic relationships using these four principal colours merging into intermediate tonal passages. Greek wall and easel painting tended to be chiefly concerned with obtaining specific effects of light and colour rather than with drawing, although the paintings on vases with strongly outlined contours would seem to refute this.

Many Roman copies of Greek statues, as well as a few surviving authentic ones, attest to the grandeur of Greek sculpture, and yet we are told that painting was its equal or even surpassed it. However, as we are without a single example to verify the written praise of painting during the classical period, our only recourse is to examine the paintings on vases and weigh the evidence.

Vessels made by potters were a part of every household. They were used for storing such substances as honey and oil and were handsomely decorated in keeping with the Greek ideal of beauty and perfection in all forms. The earliest Greek pottery style is known as the Geometric because of the type of forms painted upon it. Later, scenes of mythology, animals, and men engaged in battle or athletic contests are predominant themes—designs that revealed the Greek way of life. The greatest stylistic change occurred when an innovation in technique enabled artists to change from painting black figures on red to painting red figures on black. The workmanship on Greek vases displays a great sense of design and economy of line.

Obviously, in order to produce the great number of vessels required, there had to be assembly-line techniques of painters working in close association with potters. Since the painter's art was more time-consuming than that of the potter, doubtless the potters were gainfully employed in making endless numbers of undecorated amphorae used for transporting liquids overseas. Yet there were a number of potters who were equally skilled in the painting of their own vases.

We know that wall and panel painters of the classical period, whose names have become legend, were held in high esteem. Vase painters, on the other hand, were mostly regarded as secondary artists who at first relied mainly upon inspiration from wall and easel paintings. Later, they developed their own styles and refinements, but their names are largely unknown. Most of the signed work appears before the fifth century BC when painting on pottery was at its peak.

There is little evidence to support theories regarding the social standing of the artists at this time. The best-known sculptors were accorded considerable acclaim because the re-creation of athletes, warriors, and gods in three-dimensional form was in their hands. Statues were the manifestation of Greek civic pride and were therefore of great importance in the aesthetic life of the country.

An ostentatious display of large-scale works of architecture and art became the hallmark of Roman aspirations. Statues stood in great profusion in the city. One enormous theatre was decorated with some 3,000 statues. The Trajan victory column in the Roman forum alone was decorated with 2,500 figures sculpted in low-relief. Mural paintings on the walls of public edifices and private villas attested to the importance of art in everyday life.

A vast army of artists was engaged in the task of copying Greek works for this flourishing market in what became virtually workshop factories. Their skill and productivity added enormously to the grandeur that was Rome. A debt is owed to their integrity as craftsmen for maintaining a high standard without resorting to mass production. In some instances, the Roman copies are, in themselves, so superb that it is awesome to consider that the lost Greek originals must have been even finer in concept and realisation.

Copies made by Roman sculptors are usually distinguishable by their dependence upon additional props, such as a tree trunk or pedestal to support the weight of marble used in executing copies of bronzes. Greek casting methods also enabled them to produce bronzes of lighter weight than Roman copies in the same metal. Later restorations in which the restorers were not equal to their task deprive us of seeing the true excellence of either Greek originals or the many Roman copies.

Roman artists received few privileges when compared with philosophers, poets and writers. The fame of the greatest Greek painters and sculptors is renowned; their names are familiar to most schoolboys. The names of Roman artists, on the other hand, are hardly known. The majority of the works we possess by artists of this age remain anonymous.

Pliny records the names of a few Roman painters such as Fabius, who painted for the temple of Salus, and Turpilius, whom he curiously mentions as being left-handed. Although Turpilius was a contemporary of Pliny, he had little to write about artists of his own time. This may be due partially to the fact that he did not consider these painters to be worthy of their Greek heritage in art. He does, however, take some malicious delight in recounting the story of the painter Arellius:

> He profaned his art by a peculiar form of sacrilege. He was always in love with some woman, and he endowed the goddesses he painted with the features of his mistress. In this way we know how many mistresses he had.

Records indicate that the slaves in the households of great nobles and in the palace of the emperor were given titles commensurate with their duties in the creation or maintenance of works of art. For example, one slave might be described as *ad imagines* (to the pictures) and another as *ad statuas* (to the statues). In a sense they acted as curators and guards in homes which were the equivalent of private museums.

The basis of the organisation of the early Roman workshops was that of the father instructing his children and possibly a small number of slaves who were frequently of barbarian origin. From these humble beginnings, the workshops grew in importance to become the centres of new technology and training in the crafts.

Art as a profession had not always been considered a worthy occupation for a freeborn man in the early days of Rome. The consensus of opinion considered architecture to be the only valid art form. Under the auspices of the emperor Constantine, a stipend was granted to students of architecture together with tax concessions for those who taught architectural skills. It was not until the late Empire that organisations of men devoted to the arts were developed. Painters profited under the emperor Valentinian I by being granted exemption from certain taxes and by the free use of state-owned workshops.

CHAPTER 2

THE MEDIEVAL STUDIO

MONASTIC ART

During the period from the fourth century to the twelfth, monasteries were the chief centres for the production of art in Western Europe. The principal function of these library workshops was to make copies of the Bible and other sacred works.

In the *scriptoria*, as the workshops were called, monks trained as scribes and illuminators. Before the invention of printing, books were produced by hand, one copy at a time, and dedicated craftsmen spent their lives in the endless task of supplying Christendom with the word of God in written and pictorial form.

The monasteries, and then the cathedrals, were the training schools for artists during the Middle Ages until the establishment of art and craft guilds in the cities satisfied this need. Skilled lay brethren, who were recruited to aid in the vast undertaking of producing precious books and manuscripts, laboured over the illumination of these beautiful books with intricate designs and scrollwork on the vellum pages. These were complemented by a few superbly detailed miniature paintings, which became the source of inspiration for most easel painters in the later Middle Ages.

The word 'illumination' is taken from the Latin *illuminare*, to light. A book or manuscript in which gold in the form of leaf or paint has been used for decoration is described as illuminated. 'Miniature' is derived from the Latin verb *miniare* (to paint in red) which in earlier times described the outlining of letters and titles with the bright red pigment minium. Miniatures are found as painted illustrations in books and manuscripts or they may exist as independent paintings on a small scale.

Artists were expected to prepare book pages of the correct quality and size for calligraphy and painting. Parchment made from animal skins was the principal surface for medieval paintings as it provided a durable and receptive ground for painting and gilding as well as writing. Calf-skin was used in the production of vellum. The paints and brushes were usually made by the artists themselves who, in early days, inscribed the text as well as painting the illustrations.

Gold leaf was used to embellish the paintings and the ornate initial letters in the text. Book covers were mostly of leather and often incorporated gilding and tooling to enhance their sumptuous appearance.

Little is known about the actual workshop atmosphere of the early illuminators apart from what has been learned from a few passing references by scholars. We do know that by the beginning of the fourteenth century there were some fifteen illuminators at work in Paris in a street which was later named after them the *rue des Enlumineurs*. They established their workrooms in the vicinity of the parchment-makers and the libraries, convenient for everyone concerned.

In *Manuscripts and the Miniature*, A. Lecoy de la Marche writes:

> The illuminator [of the 14th century] is an independent worker. He exercises his occupation at home, on a table with a drawer, placed in front of a large window which affords him a good light. On this table, a desk or small easel supports the vellum over which his paint brush moves. He sits on a three-legged stool. Round him are a few phials, vases and pictures hung on the walls. His surroundings, his furniture, and his clothes appear fairly comfortable; he gives the impression of an artist who has 'arrived'.
>
> Independently of the paint-brush, he continues to use the pen; he also needs a burnisher, a sharp knife, a pair of compasses, a hare's foot and a wolf's tooth, or crystal or agate polisher to polish the surfaces, a pumice stone, pots, shells, porphyry mortars, alembics, and stoves—for most of the time he prepares his own colours. He tries them out first on a scrap of parchment; he is not familiar with the use of the palette. Then he takes the book or the leaflet he is required to illustrate and designs his work directly on it . . . the copyist has been careful to leave blank the spaces for the illuminated capitals and the miniatures, and in certain cases where he has doubted his intelligence he has indicated the initials to be designed by faint signs sketched on the extreme edge of the outer margin.
>
> The first operation consists in tracing the outlines with a pen dipped in black or brown ink, or sometimes red. Before taking his brush, the artist still uses a pen to cover certain backgrounds with hatchwork and to execute certain details such as interlacings. Then he fills in this sketch with flat colours, which he will go back over to add the shadows and modelling in darker shades.

Pictorial art, in the form of illuminated manuscripts and miniatures, dominated the early medieval period. Another function of the medieval studio was the designing of mosaics and wall murals called frescoes. These were used increasingly to convey the Christian message or as pure decoration. Some artists specialised in mosaics and the preparation and painting of walls for frescoes. Although these craftsmen emanated from the workshops, they spent most of their working days on the sites selected for the execution of their work.

Mosaic murals were made by covering a wall with a layer of fresh cement, then embedding small pieces of coloured marble or enamel. The enamel was ingeniously made by combining metallic oxides with glass paste. Gold and silver were made by gilding the cubes with leaf.

Mosaics were used by several early civilisations from the Mesopotamians to the Greeks and Romans who formed mosaics of decorative patterns on pavements and occasionally on walls. Byzantium and Ravenna were the centres for studios where craftsmen were employed to chip and shape the small cubes of coloured glass and stone and set them into patterns worked from cartoons supplied by artists. Mosaic exterior walls glistened as the sun's rays were refracted by the thousands of brilliant cubes used in their construction. In churches, the blue and gold colours created by glass and lapis lazuli captured the light from flickering candles.

The technique of true *buon fresco* painting required the application of water-based pigments which combined with the newly laid wet lime plaster to form a durable, binding film of crystalline carbonite. Speed of execution and a sureness of hand were essential, as retouching was not possible. Both Pliny and Vitruvius give details of the recipes used by the Romans which were derived from earlier Greek origins.

Fresco secco was a term given to a tempera wall painting technique in which an adhesive such as egg white or gum was mixed with pigments which were then applied to a dry plaster surface.

THE GUILD SYSTEM

During the Middle Ages associations of tradesmen called guilds were formed for the purpose of protecting the individual and maintaining standards of performance and quality.

The guild was divided into three classes. At the top were the masters, who were given the sole right to buy raw materials for working and to sell the finished product. The second class were journeymen, skilled craftsmen who worked by the day and received wages from the master and, in some instances, lived with him. The third were the beginners, or apprentices, who carried out the more menial tasks while learning their trade, and were given board and lodging in exchange for their work.

The origin and development of the system stems from the monasteries and cathedral workshops in the eleventh and twelfth centuries. In the beginning, a great deal of the building and decorating of the cathedrals and abbeys was carried out by the monks themselves, although they did employ laymen as master builders and sculptors. As a result of this early patronage, a number of talented craftsmen were raised to artistic prominence. Monastic settings provided the early training-ground for many well-known medieval artists. Hieronymus Bosch is said to have acquired his first apprenticeship, and later some of his 'hell's fire' conviction, in this atmosphere.

One might think that the painter was considered an important craftsman in the decoration of the church, but in the early Middle Ages that was not so. As mentioned previously, the creation of many works of religious significance was still the prerogative of the monks. Painters were permitted to decorate walls and carved wood, to paint banners for religious orders and to embellish heraldic shields; however, the carving of reliquaries, altarpieces, and retables was considered of greater importance. Indeed, almost all early records describe painters with the title of 'painter of images'. This stems from the fact that the cathedral painter-decorators also polychromed the reliefs and statues. In some instances they supplied the sculptor with a design for his carving. As building progressed and knowledge increased, a single artist might have gained sufficient technical skill to work as a painter, sculptor or architect.

During the period of building great cathedrals in the eleventh and twelfth centuries, the various craftsmen who were engaged in this construction and decoration often allied themselves in separate fraternities to promote their particular skills. The work sometimes passed from one generation to another. The gradual formation of the guild system provided a large degree of freedom from the church which had nourished the arts in their formative stages. The work of painting and decorating for the church and its religious orders was still carried on by craftsmen, but it was now conducted in more independent form, away from the cathedral premises, in newly established workshops supervised by a master of the craft.

Once the production of art was taken out of monastic hands and placed under guild supervision, painting tended to become more secularised and popular. A new realism based on everyday life was introduced into art and understood and appreciated by the average man.

But the emergence of painters and craftsmen from the cloisters did not mark their spiritual departure from the church. Before they had established their own guildhalls as meeting-places, the guild of painters usually assembled in their own chapels of St Luke. The members continued to support these chapels and to provide all the altar decorations, candles and religious banners for fetes and processions. New members were required to contribute a specified sum to chapel funds while apprentices might be requested to give a lump of wax for the altar candles. The religious significance of their art, undertaken in the form of commissions, was foremost in the mind of each member, whether apprentice, journeyman or master.

The accounts of painters were kept from the first day of their joining the guild until their deaths were recorded. Entered under their names was an exact account of work undertaken and its value together with credits and debits. These records are the best sources of accurate biographical information about medieval and Renaissance artists since it was compulsory for the names of all painters, other than those in the personal service of a nobleman, to be entered in the guild register.

Generally, certain types of work were placed in a standard category of payment. Set prices were observed for illuminators who supplied initial letters and small paintings for the makers of books. Paintings were priced according to the cost of the materials and the amount of time required for completion.

Payments recorded by the artist also help to assess his economic position in society. A few of these valuable documents are still in existence, providing evidence of the financial position and the remuneration in the form of fees of individual artists. A personal account book kept by Guido Reni dating from 1609, now in the possession of the Morgan Library in the United States, gives us a wealth of information regarding his personal business transactions.

In the early days of the guilds, most painters or artists were not thought of as producers of fine art, as artists are today; rather they were considered general painters and decorators without distinction as to their specialised abilities, just as they had been in the cathedral workshops. Their duties were similar in many ways to modern advertising artists or sign painters; they were paid to do a specific job.

A painter was a craftsman fulfilling an order—nothing more. However, demand was the keynote; an artist of great talent could not remain submerged forever when clients sought his personal attention. Some painters found themselves to be the new élite of their profession with established personal reputations. By the fourteenth century indications of a new attitude in guild thinking began to appear concerning the relative merits of the painters of pictures and those who worked on decorative objects only. Subsequently, the painters began to receive preferential treatment, and in nearly all large cities they were organised into their own guild.

A respect for sound craftsmanship prevailed amongst all artists. The average painter working in a guild workshop was not required to produce 'effect' pictures. Unlike many painters today, he did not strive to create works which were controversial in style or subject-matter. He was expected to produce paintings which were pleasing and uniform and, above all, technically sound so that they might last for centuries. The artist also had to know how to make the implements of his craft, such as brushes and palettes, as there were no shops from which to purchase ready-made artists' materials.

Regulations governed almost all the expendable materials used in the workshop, from the woods for panel-making to the application of gold leaf and punch patterns. The maintenance of strict control over all the articles produced benefited client and craftsman alike by ensuring a continued standard of quality.

The guilds in some towns bought materials wholesale for resale to their members. Certain guilds marked the reverse side of panels with their seal, usually to indicate their approval of the wood to be used as a painting support. Unfortunately, this was not a common practice. Had an identifying guild sign been affixed to every painting produced in the workshop, the task of generations of art historians would have been eased enormously.

The painters' guild in Flanders laid great stress upon the quality and composition of artists' pigments. Therefore, one workshop could not compete unfairly against another by using cheap colours in order to undercut production costs. As a result the Flemish paintings we see today appear in almost pristine condition, their colours nearly as rich and luminous as when they were painted.

The length of apprenticeship in the painters' guild was apparently quite variable. In Flanders a painter's apprentice might serve a term of two or three years, while elsewhere, in Italy for example, it might be as long as five to seven years. At the termination of his time, an Italian apprentice remained bound to his master for a further three years before he became a paid assistant. The sons of masters were given shorter terms of apprenticeship, however, and were also favoured by reduced taxes and lower fees. Under guild rules, a master was not allowed to accept more apprentices than he was able to train properly; the method of training was rigidly bound in a written contract or by indenture.

During his period of apprenticeship, the youth learned the skills and habits that were to remain with him for his lifetime. His future depended upon his talents as an artist, his powers of observation and retention and his adherence to the standards set by his guild. All these attributes were necessary for the apprentice to become a journeyman. One became a master only by expanding these basic qualities. The apprentice had to seek his training from those around him since art schools did not exist.

At first the apprentice learned the rudiments of his craft by performing the most menial tasks—cleaning the studio, brushes and palettes—then eventually graduating to grinding and preparing colours, and priming panels. During this time he absorbed knowledge from all that took place in the studio. He watched the master's assistants laying in compositions, painting backgrounds and details, or applying gold leaf to panels for later decoration. He learned to draw with accuracy and precision from studio casts and drapery as well as from memory. This was accompanied by studying the Bible, the various saints' legends or stories from mythology. Familiarity with these subjects was essential for a painter of the time.

As the apprentice progressed he was allowed to try his own hand at painting. These were practice pieces and not destined for the studio output. The painters often acted as teachers, criticising and encouraging the apprentice's efforts. A compliment from the master often marked the beginning of great aspirations. The young man might then be assigned to help a studio assistant lay in a composition with paint. At first he would be allowed only to paint the flat monochromatic tones of the underpainting; later he would be assigned tasks requiring greater skill.

A differentiation between the apprentice and the 'student' arose in many workshops during the Italian Renaissance. Students were placed in a rather special category as they were often the sons of noble and wealthy families. A student was given special instruction in the aesthetic concepts of art, while the workshop apprentice remained in much the same low position as in medieval times. Michelangelo, for example, entered the workshop of Ghirlandaio as an apprentice in 1448. He remained there for three years, receiving twenty-four florins, a relatively small sum in this period. Later, when he became a master, Michelangelo preferred to select students from influential families rather than hire paid assistants.

In the Florentine guild system, every man was required to have his craft membership and be a registered voter. In 1262 a document was drawn up, known as the Ordinances of Justice, which excluded nobles from guild membership. There were twenty-one guilds devoted to the crafts or arts, including those of painters, sculptors, illuminators, goldsmiths and carvers. Each had a separate house for meetings, its own officers, and the accounts of members' debits and credits. The binding ties of guild brotherhood offered protection in time of trouble, aid in financial problems, and medical relief in ill health.

The Guild of Painters in Florence was considered a minor guild, so much so that in the early fourteenth century it was incorporated into the Guild of Physicians and Apothecaries, and did not emerge again as a separate entity for nearly three centuries until, in 1563, the Academy of Design was formed. This was not as strange as it seems. The apothecaries' shops in Italy displayed a great variety of commodities for sale. In addition to equipment and sundries for medicine, they sold artists' pigments and brushes. Under the auspices of the Guild, the first illustrated books were published in Florence and sold through the apothecaries' shops, as were all the books produced at that time.

Page 35 (above) 'Egyptian Craftsmen at Work', detail from a wall-painting from the Tomb of the Two Sculptors, Thebes, about 1400 BC. (below) 'The Agony in the Garden' by Andrea Mantegna, a meticulously detailed painting on panel; the rock formations were probably painted from small stones brought into the studio

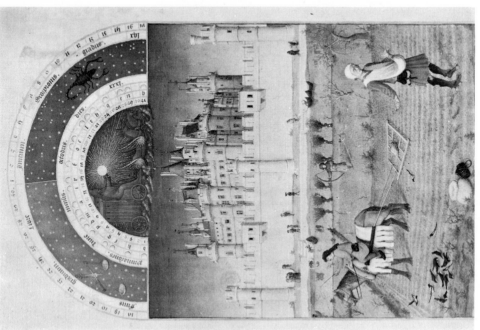

Page 36 (left) 'October' by Pol de Limbourg, from *Les Très Riches Heures du Duc de Berry* 1413–16. *(right)* 'Rinaldo and Armida with Cupids' by Anthony Van Dyck, a detail of a preliminary painting with

CHAPTER 3

THE ARTIST'S WORKSHOP

The organisation of painters into guilds in the Middle Ages led to the development of great workshops in which individual masters vied with each other to excel in the quantity of work produced in their studios. Assistants who were capable of maintaining a high standard of quality in what amounted to assembly-line techniques, were attracted to the painting factories of the greatest masters.

The master of a workshop was the final authority on the quality of the work completed by his assistants. Fortunately, not all workshop masters were the egotistical taskmasters that Benvenuto Cellini proudly claimed himself to be:

> On the morning which followed these events, I made the first step in my work upon the great salt-cellar, pressing this and my other pieces forward with incessant industry. My work-people at this time, who were pretty numerous, included both sculptors and goldsmiths. They belonged to several nations, Italian, French, and German; for I took the best I could find, and changed them often, retaining only those who knew their business well. These select craftsmen I worked to the bone with perpetual labour. They wanted to rival me; but I had a better constitution. Consequently, in their inability to bear up against such a continuous strain, they took to eating and drinking copiously; some of the Germans in particular, who were more skilled than their comrades, and wanted to march apace with me, sank under these excesses, and perished.

The relationship between master and assistant was harmonious in the main, but an assistant who was found lacking in talent or self-discipline was soon discharged. On the other hand, a truly gifted assistant was not likely to remain long in the employ of a master whose talent he surpassed.

In the late Middle Ages, the artist was not the carefree occupant of an ivory tower; he had the same problems as any businessman. The studios

3

were administered like small industries with the master as both director and sales representative, while his assistants functioned as foremen over the apprentices and pupils. The production of the studio was geared to a strict time schedule for starting and finishing various commissions. The fees charged were often based on the number of man-hours required to complete a particular work.

Fine art was produced on a highly commercial basis. Painting the same picture several times over is a practice quite abhorrent to the professional artist today; however, this was not so during the lifetime of the old masters. El Greco, for instance, produced three complete sets of identical portraits of Christ's disciples.

PRELIMINARIES TO PAINTING

Working to the dictates of a patron was the normal practice of every workshop, since painting pictures which had not been commissioned was almost unheard-of at that time. Prominent artists were less frequently subjected to the demands of their clients than were artists of lesser professional stature. They were, however, plagued by the whims and caprices of a client who wished to have changes made in a completed work. Usually an artist of repute was permitted to use his own professional judgement about a picture's subject and method of treatment; in some instances, he was required to visit the location where the completed work would finally be installed and viewed.

Once the theme of a picture and the price had been agreed upon, the contract between the patron and the artist was signed. In the initial stage, the actual planning of a pictorial composition was the prerogative of the master. Keeping both project and client in mind, he might fill his sketchbook with detailed studies of the folds of drapery, the position of hands and quick compositional layouts. Such sketches, if not used for a current commission, might serve as reference material for future works.

Fully developed drawings were often executed on toned or hand-coloured paper that served as a middle value for darks and lights which were drawn in ink or chalk or sometimes painted with watercolour and tempera. Not all drawings were sketches for planned pictures; many were created as works of art in themselves. Portraits were particularly sought after by the collectors of the day. The remarkable preservation of these works which have survived in almost pristine condition can be attributed to the fact that they were drawn on hand-made paper.

Creating a landscape background for pictures was usually a matter of invention in the studio since artists did not paint out-of-doors. Pupils were advised to draw stone blocks from which they could evolve the sometimes fantastic mountains depicted in many paintings. Cennini wrote: 'If you want to acquire a good style for mountains, and to have them look natural, get some large stone, rugged, and not cleaned up; and copy them from nature, applying the lights and the dark as your system requires.' By drawing from blocks, the mountains often resembled hewn steps. The paintings of Mantegna, 'The Agony in the Garden' (plate p. 35) in the National Gallery, London, and 'St Francis in Ecstasy' in the Frick Collection, New York, illustrate the results of following this recommendation. Besides bringing rocks and shrubs into the studio for study, some painters used wax figures to assemble table-top tableaux in order to observe the effects of light on a three-dimensional composition.

When the final drawing for the proposed picture had been completed, it was squared up. The squared projection consisted of a series of equally spaced horizontal and vertical lines drawn across the composition and intersecting at various points. This grid enabled the assistants to repeat the contents of each square of the composition on to a larger panel or canvas.

Many artists painted preliminary versions of their pictures. It was the practice in Rubens' workshop to make several small, freely painted studies, such as the 'Rinaldo and Armida with Cupids' (plate p. 36) which his assistant, Anthony Van Dyck, prepared with a visible grid for squaring up. Rubens occasionally painted more detailed versions prior to his final composition.

Large drawings prepared for wall paintings were called cartoons. These cartoons were usually on paper and were used both as a guide for tapestries and as a means of directly transferring the composition to walls for frescoes. The pattern of the cartoon was transferred to the prepared wall surface by dusting powdered chalk from a cloth bag through pinhole perforations in the paper along the drawn lines.

ETCHINGS AND ENGRAVINGS

The degree of fame achieved by a studio or particular master depended to a large extent on advertising or the circulation of evidence of their skill. Since pictures were not always available for viewing, one of the most effective methods of putting the product before the public was the publication and distribution of engravings and woodcuts. Many of these were copies after paintings that had been uniquely translated into line and tone by the graphic processes. Numerous impressions could be made from a single plate, enabling the artist to produce original images in quantities which he could sell for nominal sums. On occasion prints were exchanged between masters as examples of their work. Dürer writes of this in his diary: 'On Monday after Michaelmas 1520, I gave Thomas of Bologna a whole set of prints to send for me to Rome to another painter who should send me Raphael's work in return.' (This refers to engravings by Marcantonio Raimondi after Raphael's designs.)

Few workshop masters, apart from the great etchers and engravers of history, made their own prints. Wisely, the most renowned artists formed close relationships with outstanding engravers of their day. Raphael, who owes a part of his fame to his engraver Raimondi, and Rubens, who employed Pieter Soutman and Lucas Vorsterman, are prime examples of this type of partnership. Although most masters would have been quite capable of achieving the technical skill required in engraving and etching, the time required for these processes would have intruded on their painting production. Thus an alliance with an expert engraver was necessary to achieve an accurate interpretation of the master's designs. In order to maintain control over the work, a master often made drawings or paintings to scale as a guide for the engraver to follow, and later made corrections in pen and ink to the first proofs taken from the plate. It was the skill and dexterity of the expert engraver that brought to these copies of the masters' designs the breath of life and, not incidentally, their value.

STUDIO COPIES

Since primitive man first scratched images on the walls of caves, artists have copied works of other artists. Almost every artist has engaged in this practice; Titian copied Giorgione, and was in turn copied. Copies of paintings were often made from engravings which had originally been copied from paintings.

In their early years most artists were commissioned to copy paintings. It was common practice for collectors of the day to exchange copies of original paintings. In this way a collector could at least have an excellent replica of one of his favourite works although the original was owned by someone else.

Copies were sold to travelling artists and collectors who, when they returned to their own countries, exhibited them as examples of styles and new directions in art abroad. Painters in the North and South were made aware of the movements afoot in geographical areas that were separated by weeks of arduous travel. In such manner, the exchange of ideas generated enthusiasm for new experiments in painting.

The work of copying was not regarded as a tiresome or uninspiring task. An artist on the threshold of his career might be amply rewarded in later years for the time he had spent copying pictures of quality. Indeed, the practice of emulating the brushstrokes and colour-mixing of the masters proved to be one of the best methods of instruction for young artists. It also engendered in them an appreciation of the techniques of the more experienced and talented painters. Cennini offers sage advice in this matter:

> . . . take pains and pleasure in constantly copying the best things which you can find done by the hand of great masters. And if you are in a place where many good masters have been, so much the better for you. But I give you this advice: take care to select the best one every time, and the one who has the greatest reputation. And, as you go on from day to day, it will be against nature if you do not get some grasp of his style and of his spirit. For if you undertake to copy after one master today and after another one tomorrow, you will not acquire the style of either one or the other, and you will inevitably, through enthusiasm, become capricious, because each style will be distracting your mind. You will try to work in this man's way today, and in the other's tomorrow, and so you will not get either of them right. If you follow the course of one man through constant practice, your intelligence would have to be crude indeed for you not to get some nourishment from it. Then you will find, if nature has granted you any imagination at all, that you will eventually acquire a style individual to yourself, and it cannot help being good; because your hand and your mind, being always accustomed to gather flowers, would ill know how to pluck thorns.

Copies have been made which have equalled and on some occasions almost surpassed the original. This is not unreasonable, as many of the copyists were destined to become great masters, while some of the works they copied were by artists of lesser stature whose names are relatively unknown today.

Imitating the style of a master was for centuries the means of training young artists, and inevitably it led to even the most outstanding artists being influenced. Cennini tells us that Raphael imitated his master Perugino so exactly that it was impossible to distinguish one from the other.

In many instances copies of works of the old masters are the only evidence we have of missing or destroyed pictures. A copy by Battista Franco of

Michelangelo's destroyed 'Noli Me Tangere' shows us what a beautiful painting the original must have been. Occasionally a copy is found as a painting within a painting. Painted backgrounds of room interiors with miniature replicas can be used by art historians for the purpose of identifying and dating the works of other masters. In a painting of an Antwerp home by Frans Francken the Younger, the artist depicts Rubens' painting 'Samson and Delilah' hanging over a fireplace.

One of the finest painters of paintings was David Teniers the Younger, who was Court Painter to the Regent of the Netherlands, the Archduke Leopold, a great collector of paintings. Teniers was appointed keeper of the archduke's collection and during the seventeenth century produced for him at least eight 'Painted Galleries' (plate p. 53). They depict all of the pictures in the archduke's collection (the majority of which were Italian) copied in miniature. This recorded series offers visual proof of paintings that existed at the time and has been instrumental in helping historians to identify and date many of them. Artists sometimes recorded their paintings in other pictorial forms. For example, Claude recorded his paintings in a group of drawings called the 'Liber Veritatis', now in the British Museum. He thus hoped to ensure the identification of his works should they be either lost or stolen.

TRADEMARKS

Stamped signs or monograms were the trademarks of particular workshops. These signs did not denote that the work was from the hand of a specific master, but rather that it had been produced in his workshop either partially or totally with the help of assistants. These marks were a confirmation of the approval of the master, just as a guild stamp was used to affirm the quality of wood used for panels.

The studio of Cranach employed a stamp depicting a serpent on panel paintings. In later centuries other devices were used for identification in the composition of the paintings themselves. Whistler, for example, used a butterfly monogram on his works. The contemporary British artist Terence Cuneo paints a mouse into his pictures, while more than one artist has used his thumb print in wet paint to ensure that his work is distinguishable from possible forgeries.

COPIES AND FORGERIES

Popular painters of every age have been imitated. Indeed, the absence of students and amateurs desirous of copying his work might worry an established artist; however, an artist who suffers financially because of these attempts might be less tolerant of his imitators. Van Mander, writing about the Flemish painter Hans Bol relates: 'At Antwerp, Bol stopped painting on fabric because he found out that people bought his canvases, copied them and then sold them as originals. He began to paint landscapes and little scenaries in miniature style, saying: "Let those who can imitate me now, whistle on their fingers." '

A painter who sets out to copy an Old Master may succeed in obtaining a surface veneer and he may display a clever technical achievement in creating almost identical materials and suggesting great age, but he can never capture the sensitivity of the underpainting or the spirit in which the original creator conceived his composition and applied his paint. The copyist cannot re-create the thought processes of an artist who lived centuries earlier. The copyist can only attempt to emulate superficially the surface quality of a picture; he must, of necessity, work in a tightly controlled manner that lacks the inspiration and sureness of the original painter.

The longer the interval between completion of an original picture and the making of a copy, the more noticeable the differences. Pictures copied in the studios of great masters have not only the advantage of age consistent with the original, but also that of having been copied by artists with attitudes and experiences similar to those of the master.

A picture becomes a forgery only when the intention of copying is replaced by the intention of deceiving a prospective purchaser. Many pictures which were innocently painted and declared as copies have been labelled forgeries because their owner attempted to pass them off at a later date as originals.

Two different approaches have been used by forgers. Some have chosen to copy certain works from the most familiar and popular period of a master's career. Others attempt to imitate the early style of a master and create a totally new work rather than copy one already in existence.

Present-day methods of scientific examination of paintings can cast serious doubt on what may appear to be genuine pictures that are both well documented and, in the opinion of experts, original. The surface of a suspected spurious painting may be studied under magnification to establish that the handling of the brushwork only vaguely resembles the technique of the master. Through the use of X-rays and infra-red photography, the deliberate forger's inability to reproduce what he cannot see is revealed in the brushstrokes of the underpainting. In all cases of paintings classified as copies or forgeries that have been examined by these methods, the underpainting may be seen as inconsistent with that of the original.

Perhaps the most illustrious artist to have engaged in copying with deception in mind was Michelangelo. Vasari relates the following story:

> But it was no wonder that Michelangelo was so able. He studied continually. He copied a copper engraving by the German Martin Schongauer. The subject was Saint Anthony tormented by devils. First he drew it in pen and ink and then he painted it. He studied actual fish scales to make the devil's scales more real. He also copied drawings of the old masters so perfectly that his copies could not be distinguished from the originals, since he smoked and tinted the paper to give it the appearance of age. He was often able to keep the originals and return his copies in their stead. He did this only because of his admiration for the old masters.

Fortunately, in the history of art there have been relatively few artists who have turned to forgery.

A picture may be universally admired and deemed to be worth a considerable amount of money one day, and the next day be reduced to nothingness by the pronouncement of an expert that it is a forgery. The question arises —is the picture itself any the less satisfactory? It should not be; however, with the loss of association, the picture becomes relatively worthless and joins the ranks of uncherished fakes. Yet even a fraudulent painting may have value; for instance, the forgeries by Hans van Meegeren of Vermeer and other Dutch masters which, after his exposure and trial in 1947, were considered worthless and an embarrassment to their owners, have begun to fetch modestly high prices as celebrated forgeries.

BORROWING

Artists have borrowed whole compositions or details from earlier painters and graphic artists. Throughout the history of art, painters have used the designs of others, not just to copy, but as the inspiration for new and original works translated into their own style. An example is Manet, who based his 'Olympia' on Titian's idealised painting of the mythical Venus. Manet is said to have used a woman of the streets as a model to portray the classically reclining goddess.

ATTRIBUTIONS

The studio workshop establishment has presented art historians with many ambiguities on which to ponder. For generations opinion has been divided as to whether a picture was painted wholly or only in part by a particular master; the workshop practice of producing several versions of one picture has resulted in confusion over which painting is the original.

Many historians have agreed to disagree about the absolute authorship of certain paintings and have generalised by ascribing them to particular workshops, to schools of painting, or to followers and imitators. Attributions appearing in many art gallery catalogues are based on a simple code which is often misunderstood. W. G. Constable, in his book, *The Painter's Workshop*, gives the following definitions:

> The term 'By X' implies that the work is for the most part by the master's hand. 'By X and assistants', suggests considerably more help, though the master plays the dominant part; while 'Studio of X' generally means that though the conception of the painting is that of X, that he supervised the execution, may have done a limited amount of work on it, and was paid for it, yet the work is largely by other hands. 'School of X', however, implies elimination of X from the work itself, but that the painter of the picture worked under his influence, following him in ideas, conventions, and technical methods. At the same time, some degree of contact with X is implied, though not necessarily that the painter was a pupil of his. In this, the term differs from 'Follower of X' which may well be used of a painter of considerable later date than X, though he has modelled his work on that of X. Distinct, again, is 'Imitator of X' which suggests a more slavish follower, with no independent ideas. This, however, has a different connotation from 'After X', which is used of a copy, with or without variations.

A painting bearing the name of the Master of Liège, for example, signifies that certain documentary or stylistic evidence exists which indicates that it is the work of a painter whose name is unknown, but who probably worked in Liège during a certain period. An unknown master may be credited by art historians with several paintings or perhaps only a single picture. Paintings thus ascribed await the discovery of new documentation or evidence from scientific investigatory methods to support or disprove their origins. When new information is added to what already exists, this is cross-linked with other sources of reference and may help to evolve a new theory about the artist and the picture.

Claims and counter-claims rage about the authorship of certain paintings. Practically all the masters have suffered from erroneous attributions; consequently some art historians and critics have become over-zealous in attempting to correct mistakes of the past. Attributions of dubious validity will continue to be challenged as long as art exists.

Today laboratories specialising in art conservation are continuing to make new discoveries concerning the technical aspects of paintings and are providing useful information on which art historians can base their conclusions for attributions.

Texts written about a particular master become outdated through the discovery of a new painting acknowledged to be his. Thus the total number of known pictures produced by an artist may fluctuate. The recent discovery of a painting 'The Dice Players' by Georges La Tour raised the total number of pictures acknowledged to be from his hand to twenty-nine. A week later, another La Tour was reported to have been found, possibly as a result of the considerable amount of publicity accorded the first. On the other hand, an artist's verified total output may be decreased by proving attributions to be mistaken. At one time there were a few hundred pictures attributed to Leonardo da Vinci; today there are only fifteen listed as authenticated—the rest are more accurately described as copies, or by his school, or by followers and imitators.

FOLLOWERS

The number of artists who desire to follow in the steps of a master attests to his accomplishments and perpetuates his name. The seal of a master is indelibly stamped upon those students and followers who strive to echo his style. Caravaggio is an example of an artist who attracted a large school of followers. His innovative concepts and revolutionary style in painting affected artists of his own and succeeding generations.

Merely copying a work of a particular artist does not make the copyist a follower. A true follower must be imbued with an inner conviction approaching near-reverence for the work and even the life-style of his ideal. Raphael generated this veneration in many artists who became his devoted followers through the centuries.

Almost all of the great artists studied under a master; they joined the guilds and became masters themselves, employing assistants and influencing followers. Knowledge was passed on, with each succeeding generation finding new ways of improving materials, techniques and recipes. In their formative years, all artists have sought a dominating influence to follow; emulating the style of an admired master has been the basis of all learning in art. It was only the less talented and unimaginative painters, unable to develop their own style, who remained for ever classified as followers.

CHAPTER 4

PATRONAGE

PATRON – A wretch who supports with insolence and is paid with
flattery.

Dr Samuel Johnson in a letter to the
Earl of Chesterfield, 1775

The inspiration and pleasure derived from the arts and letters has often
prompted individuals or groups to offer active encouragement and financial assistance to artists, and such patronage has played a significant role in
influencing the development of art over the centuries.

Some patrons adopted a cavalier attitude towards the artist, seeing him
merely as the means by which their own ideas might be implemented.
Others recognised the genius they were instrumental in cultivating, but few
expressed the enthusiasm that Cellini immodestly records:

> I carried with me the wax model which I had made in Rome at the
> Cardinal of Ferrara's request. When I appeared again before the King
> and uncovered my piece, he cried out in astonishment: 'This is a
> hundred times more divine a thing than I had ever dreamed of. What
> a miracle of a man! He ought never to stop working.'

The artist has occasionally been regarded as being at the mercy of the
patron who might attempt to extract from him the maximum of talent and
effort with the minimum of compensation. Yet it was often the patron who
was placed in the onerous position of having to implore and cajole an artist
to finish a commission he had undertaken. The relationship was not always
happily fulfilled; patrons might not live to see their commissions realised
and artists sometimes died before completing their work. Projects were
often begun by one craftsman and finished by another after his death.

In the days when art patronage was dominated mainly by the religious orders, rich feudal barons and merchants commissioned works for the church in which they were shown in pious poses, kneeling at the foot of the cross or in attendance as wise men in a manger scene. At first the donor was depicted in a painting assuming an insignificant role, but later he became a dominant figure in many compositions, rivalling in size and strategic placement the divine beings themselves. As a donor to the church, the patron not only enhanced his prestige in the community, but also, it was hoped, ensured his place in the life hereafter. An integral part of patronage was making the populace aware of these acts of generosity.

Patronage, indeed, has not always been conducted in a selfless light. The deep-rooted aspirations of many patrons to achieve lasting glory for themselves have, on several occasions, succeeded remarkably. The outstanding patron of the twelfth century, about whom documentation exists, was Abbot Suger of the abbey of St-Denis in France. His impeccable taste and zeal for artistic splendour were unparalleled in his age. The noted art scholar Francis Haskell says of him:

> From all over France he summoned stonemasons, carpenters, painters, and goldsmiths. But while he held that windows, sculpture, furnishings and jeweled objects could all help the soul visualize the celestial hierarchies, he was also prompted by another motive, one which has often played a leading role in patronage: the desire to perpetuate his own fame. Everywhere in the church he so splendidly decorated he had his name prominently displayed, and in the embellishment of St Denis one encounters the first notable instance of that strange combination of personal ambition and reverence which was to recur frequently thereafter.

CONTRACTS

It was normal for a contract to be drawn up between the artist and patron when commissioning any large-scale work. Under the terms of such a contract, the artist would usually be advised of the subject he was to paint and its size. The artist, for his part, would probably wish to see the intended site so that he might judge for himself the prevailing light and surroundings in which the picture would eventually be displayed.

Contracts would sometimes stipulate that the master should carry out the work himself. In consequence, commissions were undertaken by the master which, under other circumstances, he might have delegated almost entirely to his assistants. In his letters, Rubens makes particular note of the degree to which his own hand was used in painting various pictures. A contract might require the use of specific colours of a certain quality or designate the number of full-length figures to be included in the composition, for which the artist was paid accordingly. Giotto, who was renowned in his lifetime, received exceptionally high recompense for his work; of course, he had a large entourage of assistants to whom he paid wages from his fee. However, Giotto was an élite member of the painting fraternity. More often, fees were small and sometimes remuneration was quite poor, considering the artist's skill and the time taken to complete a commission.

Payment to the artist was often made in three stages: a deposit to guarantee the commission, an additional payment when the work was in progress, and a final payment upon completion of the undertaking. Payment was not always agreed by contract; on occasion the painter was merely assured that he would be generously rewarded. A surprising number of painters found such terms acceptable when the patrons were persons of wealth and importance. Sometimes a painter did not receive a reward in keeping with his work but, rather than risk the displeasure of an illustrious client, he judiciously accepted the offering and remained silent. By recommending him to others, an important patron could be invaluable to a young painter.

A record of all contracts undertaken by the artist had to be entered in the guild's books. Any dispute arising between a patron and an artist was investigated and settled by officers of the guild. Perhaps the greatest cause of disagreement was determining the amount of time a commissioned project would take. Historical documents and letters concerning the discord that arose owing to the failure of the painter to deliver a completed picture when agreed make up a good deal of available documentary evidence. J. M. Fletcher, in an article in the *Burlington Magazine*, published an exchange of letters between Isabella d'Este, an intermediary for Michele Vianello, and Giovanni Bellini, from which the following extracts are taken.

Isabella to Vianello   10 March 1501
She wants Bellini's price reduced to 100 ducats eighteen months seems too long to her as she wants Bellini's picture completed in a year. Bellini still has to work in the Doge's Palace but as he is a good master he will be able to find the time. She will close the deal at 100 ducats and she will be satisfied if he finishes it in one year.

Giovanni Bellini to Isabella   2 July 1504
On bended knee he asks her forgiveness for the delay which was due to the press work and not to any neglect of her orders which are engraved in his heart. If his work doesn't satisfy her great wisdom and experience it must be attributed to the limitations of his ability.

This flowery and contrite letter seems to have warmed her heart, and further letters attest to her receiving the picture and to her final satisfaction, despite the delay.

An artist whose work was in demand frequently undertook more commissions than either he or his assistants could adequately handle. The master, responsible for the livelihood of a large retinue of helpers, was loath to refuse commissions for fear they would not be as numerous during times of economic decline. Thus the backlog of work would continue to mount while clients fumed and complained of long delays in receiving their commissioned works.

Few artists can predict how a painting will progress. A painting may have been abandoned as unsuccessful after considerable time and effort had been expended, necessitating a fresh start. True patronage demands patience and a rather special aptitude for understanding the desire for perfection inherent in most artists.

ARTISTIC INDEPENDENCE

In the early Middle Ages not every painter was a member of a guild, nor was he employed in the workshop of a master; some became attached to the household of a patron. A painter who was taken into the service of a patron was dependent upon that patron for food, lodging and a monetary stipend. In turn, the artist was expected to work exclusively for his patron, although on occasion he was encouraged to paint for the patron's friends. Such an appointment could prove inhibiting, but this was often compensated for by promotion to a higher post and salary within the official establishment of household employees. In addition, the patron might pay for journeys by the painter for the purpose of broadening his artistic horizons. Not the least of the benefits was the opportunity to meet wealthy and influential people who, by their interest in his work, could make the painter's name familiar in still wider circles.

Although patronage released the artist from financial worries as his prestige increased, he sometimes found the ties that bound him to a single patron restrictive. The important lucrative commissions offered by others might prove irresistibly tempting to an artist of ability who wished to advance in his profession. A compromise might be arranged with the employer whereby the artist would secure his own lodgings and studio from which he could accept work on a competitive basis, while still receiving a small subsidy from his patron.

Not all painters continued to work strictly by commission. In order to maintain their overheads, a few began to paint pictures of their own conception on speculation during periods when commissions were not forthcoming. These would be shown and sold to prospective clients who visited their studios. Some artists made drawings of proposed pictures, while others sketched compositions on canvas in outline which they offered to paint and complete for customers.

The work of a great master was in sufficient demand to warrant his independence from clients who restricted his vision. An artist who was a creative genius could not bear working to the dictates of patrons who were neither eminent nor understanding. Overseeing the workmanship of a large staff of helpers and conforming to guild regulations did not appeal to an individualist who preferred to produce fewer works and have them be of his own creation. Vasari illustrates this with a story about Michelangelo painting in the Sistine Chapel:

> Michelangelo now began to prepare the cartoons for the ceiling. His Holiness ordered that the paintings by the older masters of the time of Pope Sixtus should be effaced. Michelangelo's fee was put at fifteen thousand ducats, an estimate made by Giuliano da Sangallo. But the extent of the work compelled Michelangelo to seek assistance. He sent to Florence for Granacci, Giuliano Bugiardini, Jacopo di Sandro, and the elder Indaco, with Agnolo da Donnino, and Aristotile da Sangallo. These men were experienced in fresco-painting. Michelangelo, stimulated by the challenge, resolved to prove his pre-eminence. He finished the drawings but deferred beginning the painting until his assistants should arrive.
>
> The masters reached the city and the work was begun. Michelangelo gave them a portion to do by way of sample. What they did came far from approaching his expectations or fulfilling his purpose. One morning he decided to destroy the whole of it. He then shut himself up alone in the chapel and not only refused them admittance, but would not see any of them at his house. Finally, ashamed and mortified, they returned to Florence. Michelangelo made arrangements to do the whole thing himself.

PATRONAGE IN ITALY

Italian patronage of the arts in the later Middle Ages owed a great deal to rivalry amongst religious orders in the church as well as to rivalry between cities. The Florentines, for example, were vying to erect churches that were more splendidly decorated than those of the Romans, while the Jesuits and

Page 53 (above) 'Printing', an engraving by Abraham Bosse. The interior of a seventeenth century French printmaker's studio; one man turns the wheel of an etching press while another wipes ink from a metal plate; a third grinds pigments beneath prints hung up to dry. (below) 'The Picture Gallery of Archduke Leopold Wilhelm' by David Teniers, a fine example of one of Teniers' paintings documenting great collections

Page 54 'The Procession of the Magi' by Benozzo Gozzoli, a fresco commissioned by Piero de'Medici for

the Capuchins sought prominence as patrons. Most of the wealth in this period was in the hands of the church and the nobility. Self-seeking individuals in both spheres devoted themselves to outdoing each other in providing sumptuous decorations and furnishings for their palaces and great houses.

By the seventeenth century, papal patronage of the arts in Italy had assumed a virtual monopoly over the most celebrated artistic talents of the time. A number of artists were engaged in the secular pre-occupation of painting and sculpting papal portraits for various churches. Indeed, if travellers in Italy wished to see the best of 'modern art', they were obliged to visit the churches.

Monumental projects of decoration had been largely the province of papal patronage. With the increased wealth of leading clergy members and prominent Roman families, however, numerous large-scale works were commissioned by them, while the grandiose decorative schemes and overall power of the popes declined. For example, Cardinal Sefaneschi commissioned many superb decorations which adorn St Peter's in Rome.

The decline in the number of new churches and palaces constructed in the late seventeenth century reduced the availability of prospective commissions. Competition among artists was further heightened by the increase in the number of members in the profession. Italian and foreign artists working in Rome, which ranked as the most cosmopolitan city in Europe, nearly reached a point of saturation. However, patronage by important families increased and official commissions were sufficient to ensure that the workshops of talented artists remained steadily productive for some time.

PATRONAGE IN THE NETHERLANDS

In the Netherlands patronage developed along rather different lines. In writing about Dutch patronage in the seventeenth century, Francis Haskell concludes: 'Apart from the intense commercialisation of art—unparalleled elsewhere in Europe until the nineteenth or even twentieth century—the most conspicuous contribution of the Dutch to art patronage, was the group commission.' Professional associations such as those of the military, merchants and surgeons commissioned their portraits as groups. Painting these and other well-to-do members of the various guilds in the Netherlands occupied Rembrandt, Hals, Jordaens and many others. Two outstanding examples of large group portraits are Rembrandt's famous 'The Night

4

Watch', or, more correctly, 'The Military Company of Captain Frans Banning Cocq', and Hals' 'Banquet of the Archers of St George'.

Painting several portraits in one picture required the artist to schedule a series of appointments. Rather than having the entire group arrive in a body in their Sunday best, as they would for a portrait in a photographer's studio today, individuals came for sittings and were arranged into the composition. In some instances placement was accorded by rank, although more prominent positioning and fully detailed modelling was sometimes secured by an increased payment to the artist.

Dutch painters began to develop new subject-matter by the observation of their surroundings before their counterparts in the South. While this new and realistic concept of art based on contemporary life held sway in Holland, Italian artists in guild workshops were still carrying out elaborate commissions for the church and the great families. Almost all their work still embodied the religious themes of the past.

The slackening of official commissions and the lack of interest of Holland's rather austere Protestant church brought about the first large-scale support of artists by the middle classes. Rich Dutch burghers and prosperous farmers, who were the *nouveaux riches*, still retained their pedestrian attitudes. Their tastes in pictorial art were conditioned by their bourgeois background; landscapes with animals, family portraits, house interiors, ribald scenes and ultra-realistic still lifes were the genres they preferred. The painters, in turn, pandered to their clients' desires with all the skill to be expected of the inheritors of a great tradition of sound craftsmanship. Never before had such commonplace subjects as cattle been made the principal subjects in so many landscape compositions. The paintings of Albert Cuyp, for example, became much sought after by Dutch farmers who enjoyed his homely and familiar scenes.

The prevailing artistic atmosphere of the seventeenth century in the Low Countries was far removed from that depicted in the religiously austere hell-fire paintings of the Middle Ages. This new irreverence is illustrated by Van Mander's story of his contemporary, the Flemish painter Hans Fredeman de Vries, who made a speciality of painting immaculately detailed architecture and perspective views. It seems that Vries was commissioned to paint a view of a summerhouse in perspective, and, to add to its beauty, he painted an open door in the picture. One day Pieter Bruegel paid Vries a visit only to find him away. Taking up a brush, Bruegel painted a coarse peasant in a soiled shirt engaged in intimate relations with a peasant woman. The incident so provoked laughter in those who saw it that Vries' patron declared he would not have the painting altered for any amount of money.

A new class of dealers began to attend to the demand for small easel pictures for the home and set up shops and galleries from which they sold the works of artists they represented. At first the dealers bought pictures and then resold them for a profit. Later, they took paintings on commission, sharing the price received with the artist or returning the paintings if unsold.

ROYAL PATRONAGE

The church, represented by Popes Urban VIII and Alexander VII and Cardinals Richelieu and Mazarin, vied with the royal personages of King Louis XIV of France, King Charles I of England, and Philip IV of Spain in obtaining the services of the finest painters and sculptors in Europe. During the seventeenth century, royalty began to monopolise the role of grand patron of the arts, a position long held by the church.

Rulers, whether they were artistically inclined or not, recognised the prestige value of appointing artists to their courts and commissioning extravagant projects which would enhance their own reputations. Many a monarch brooded when he could not obtain the services of a favoured artist, although those already in royal employ were often restricted from working for anyone else. The status of a court painter soon rose to unprecedented heights.

Rubens, Holbein, Velasquez, Goya and many other great masters were at one time or another appointed to official posts as court painters. In some instances, the appointment was made to honour visiting painters while they were engaged in fulfilling particular commissions for royal patrons. Several painters, respected for their intellect as well as their artistic talents, became popular by establishing friendships with exalted members of the royal family, thereby incurring the enmity of less favoured members of court. Velasquez spent many years in the service of Philip IV after having attained a high office. Unfortunately, the duties of court life often intruded for long periods upon his creative time, thus depriving the world of a larger number of works by this Spanish master.

In addition to painting the varied commissions of a royal patron and portraits of court members, an artist might be sent to the widely separated kingdoms of Europe for the purpose of painting prospective marriage partners. Examples of such portraits are Holbein's 'Christina of Denmark, Duchess of Milan' and 'Anne of Cleves' which he painted for Henry VIII.

Accuracy and truthfulness were paramount for the successful portrait painter of this period who might easily lose his head by endowing a rather plain bride-elect with physical attributes she did not possess.

Besides inviting artists to court, royal patrons and collectors such as Francis I of France, Philip II of Spain and Charles I of England employed art agents in various countries. The agents' duties included arranging commissions or direct purchases with outstanding masters, informing them of the intrigues of rival collectors and searching for little-known but talented painters. The safe transport of completed works by land and sea was an additional responsibility of the agent.

By the seventeenth century, interest in commissioning great works no longer held a fascination for the illustrious. The art of the time did not seem to compare with that of the Renaissance. New concepts in art seemed inferior to past traditions. The long-awaited revival of that golden age had failed to materialise and patronage drifted into the acquisition of the Old Masters and antiquities. Art became a commodity of the sale-rooms and dealers profited; prospective clients tended to ignore the work of living artists—a situation which continues to exist today.

NEW CONCEPTS

The decline of grand-scale commissions from munificent patrons was responsible for the emergence of a new concept in the art world. Direct contracts between the patron and the artist in his studio began to be replaced by arrangements involving a middleman who organised the display of paintings on his own premises and invited potential buyers to view them. This new type of art transaction began in Holland and spread to Italy, France, and the rest of the Continent. Both the painter and the collector began to conduct their business through a dealer who deducted a share of the price achieved and offered his services to both parties.

On the Continent, art dealers and galleries rapidly became the established intermediaries between clients and artists. In England, however, the eighteenth century heralded the greatest period of English patronage. The English tended to support the theory that anything foreign was exotic and therefore desirable, while patronage of native-born artists was largely confined to commissions of portraits and landscapes.

Patronage may appear in many different guises. It may come from a member of the artist's family who believes in his talents or it may come from a complete stranger. The wife, working in order to support an artist husband and perhaps a family so that he may prove himself in a profession that has few financial rewards, is an exemplary form of patronage.

One of the most loyal of all patrons of the arts must surely be Theo Van Gogh whose own small income as an art dealer was reduced considerably by his generosity to his brother Vincent, enabling him to continue painting. Money alone does not altogether suffice; Theo's letters of encouragement undoubtedly sustained Vincent who might well have taken his life earlier had this loving relationship not existed.

The advent of the Impressionist movement opened a new era in which the patron was exposed to the same abuses as the artist. Outstanding among those who supported the Impressionists through this tumultuous period, in which they were castigated by the public, as well as by members of their own profession, were Victor Choquet, Père Tanguy, Georges Charpentier and the dealer-patrons Vollard, Durand-Ruel and Kahnweiler. The quiet, dedicated confidence of Victor Choquet, who helped poverty-stricken painters although he had little money himself, proved that patronage need not always be a matter of wealth and self-indulgence.

CHAPTER 5

STUDIOS AND EQUIPMENT

The painter's studio has changed slowly over the last few centuries; however, the basic requirements of good light and painting materials of quality have endured. Improvements in the essential equipment and the introduction of new aids provide the artist with all his material needs.

Before the seventeenth century, only the artist was concerned about improving his equipment. Today manufacturers cater to his every desire. Indeed, the modern artist has an often bewildering choice of products at his disposal; there is practically nothing he need make that has not already been provided. Yet this very ease and convenience has been ultimately responsible for the loss of concern for sound craftsmanship and knowledge of the permanency of materials. The Old Masters who prepared their own supports and colours attained an affinity with these materials and this knowledge was passed on from generation to generation.

A sound technique is essential for the lasting preservation of a work of art. Progress can be achieved only by close study of and respect for the proven methods of the past.

THE STUDIO ENVIRONMENT

The majority of studios have been within or adjoining the artist's own dwelling. A close proximity to their work has enabled artists to utilise their periods of creativity more efficiently. A specially constructed studio is the ideal, but through the ages artists have had to make do with the environment Fate and Fortune have given them.

Painters' studios naturally varied one from the other. In some Flemish studio workshops, the master worked in the same room as his assistants, but a few preferred to work in adjoining rooms. Rembrandt, according to the inventory of his lodgings, gave separate rooms to each of his pupils.

The workshops of Italy contrasted with those of the North in both organisation and appearance. Flemish workshops produced paintings principally for the burghers and rich merchants: Italian workshops were directed in the main towards the greater glory of the Church.

A large Italian workshop might combine the talents of architects, sculptors, metalsmiths, painters and decorators under a master with experience in several allied arts. An apprentice in such a workshop could acquire knowledge from the various specialists in their crafts. In some workshops foundries were established for casting sculpture and shaping ecclesiastical objects. Occasionally, all these talents were manifest in a single individual. Michelangelo, Leonardo, Cellini and Verrocchio are outstanding examples of the high degree of attainment artists achieved during the Renaissance.

Prior to the nineteenth century, studios were seldom the domain of disorderly Bohemians; they were clean and tidy working establishments. The individual habits of one painter might differ from those of his colleagues, but a Jackson Pollock, ankle-deep in litter, would not have been tolerated. Slovenly work habits were curbed for the good of all workshop members.

A typical Dutch studio of the seventeenth century was established in a brick-fronted dwelling. If the studio were on the ground floor, it was more than likely paved with stone or with the tiles we see in paintings of the more elegant interiors of that period. If it were above ground level, the floor would be of wood. The rough walls were usually whitewashed to reflect the light.

Dutch realist painters developed a fascination for their own comfortable middle-class surroundings, depicting them as backgrounds in numerous pictures. We encounter the same objects and props in various works of the same artist. A maid servant may be seen holding a pitcher that has been used previously in another painting, while a cavalier sits on a familiar chair beside a table on which are placed objects cherished by the painter.

LIGHTING

Natural northern light entering the studio from a side window was the preferred lighting arrangement for almost all painters, as it kept the sun from falling directly upon their work or, in the case of a portrait painter, upon the model. Sunlight streaming through a window on to a picture in progress was undesirable. To reduce glare, an oiled paper was sometimes stretched across the window to diffuse the harsh light; curtains and drapes were used extensively to adjust the amount of light required. Several paintings of Dutch studio interiors are shown with windows draped in this manner.

In an article 'The Life of a Dutch Artist in the Seventeenth Century' (*Burlington Magazine*, 1905, beginning in Vol 7), Dr W. Martin states:

> The most advantageous light was to be obtained in studios with a large window divided into four squares, with two openings in each square which could be closed or opened at will. The most varied effects of light were obtainable in this way; it was possible, for instance, to let the full light fall on the canvas and to leave the model in a more subdued light. Again the lower half of the window could be entirely closed, while the model remained in a high light without disturbing reflections from the outside.

Because of the limitations of glassmaking techniques during the Middle Ages, window panes were quite small. Ateliers with great skylights and side windows had yet to be constructed.

The working day was from sunrise to sunset, so that the number of hours spent at work each day differed in summer and winter, a disparity which would hardly be tolerated in a commercial studio today. An artist of great inspiration, however, could not be restricted to working only during the daylight hours. Vasari tells us:

> Michelangelo slept little and often got up in the night to resume his labors with the chisel. For these occasions he had made a cap of pasteboard, in the centre of which he placed his candle, which thus gave him light without encumbering his hands.

We are told that Rembrandt, who was the son of a miller, created in his paintings the dramatic effects of illuminated figures against dark backgrounds after observing shafts of light falling from the high window upon men in the mill interior.

The studio window has often inspired artists as part of the subject-matter of their paintings and has been widely used as a device for creating a feeling of space and distance. In many instances, the window has been a vantage-point from which the artist has observed exterior surroundings such as gardens or distant landscapes. The French artist Utrillo and many others have painted compositions from their studio windows. Usually the windows were at least a floor above ground level, giving the painter a bird's-eye view and the opportunity to employ three-point perspective, a challenge to any serious artist.

THE STUDIO PORTRAYED IN ART

The fascination of artists throughout history for leaving some pictorial evidence of their studios and equipment has preserved for us a remarkable record of information. The Egyptians left wall paintings illustrating artists, sculptors and goldsmiths pursuing their crafts. The illuminators and miniature painters of the Middle Ages have also recorded their daily working lives. In some instances this was done in an amusing manner with the illustrations emphasising the trials and tribulations of their chosen professions. Craftsmen in the allied arts of tapestry, weaving, glassmaking and ceramics are shown engaged in the progressive stages of their trades.

The interiors of graphic art studios were often depicted in drawings and etchings. These have provided much information as to the type of presses, specialised tools and working methods of various early workshops.

MATERIALS AND TECHNIQUES OF PAINTING

The tradition of Gothic painting, which flourished in the Low Countries during the Middle Ages, was slowly replaced by a new realism. The formal elegance of the Gothic style had compensated for its often static, two-dimensional representation. Artists later sought to achieve a more lifelike effect by developing an illusory third dimension in their paintings.

The realisation of this new three-dimensional concept was greatly aided by technical advances in the studio. The discovery and use of oil as a medium was one of the most important in the history of art.

The luminosity of the colours of early Flemish paintings had been achieved by using smooth, lustre-white gesso panel surfaces which were painted upon with pigments of quality and stable binding substances. The paints were sometimes applied in a glazing technique of thinly dispersed colours, one over the other or in cross-hatched strokes.

Most of the limited number of colours available at this time were obtained from minerals which, when combined with egg, tended to harden with enamel-like brilliance, remaining relatively untarnished by the passage of time.

Egg tempera paintings on wooden panels prepared by the application of successive layers of white chalk, mixed with size and polished to a glossy finish with an agate stone, have retained their original vividness to a remarkable degree. In the hands of a great master the egg medium was unrivalled for obtaining splendid detail. However, the slow and methodical technique of tempera painting imposed a restriction upon artists who wanted a more facile method which would enable them to increase the volume of their work.

The invention of oil painting has been generally credited to the fifteenth-century Flemish painter Jan van Eyck. Although there is considerable evidence that other painters had been employing oil-based painting media before van Eyck, it is agreed that he achieved the most significant results.

The introduction of powder pigments bound in oil gave painting a greater range of possibilities. With the addition of various binders, the paints could be applied in completely opaque layers or in superimposed transparent glazes, giving greater translucency and depth to the composition. Some notable painters employed both techniques together on a single canvas. Rubens, for example, contrasted areas of thinly diluted colours, similar to watercolour in consistency, with thickly opaque passages spread with a stiff brush and later blended with glazes. A larger surface could be covered more rapidly in oil paint than had been possible with the egg tempera medium.

The technique of applying paints varied from century to century and from one workshop to another. The traditional technique of building up a painting, layer over layer, to achieve a variety of tonal values was adhered to by the Old Masters. It was not until the nineteenth century that new concepts in art changed measurably. What hitherto might have been considered merely a sketch, or at best a preparatory underpainting, might now be judged as a complete and satisfying work of art in itself.

The *alla prima* method of applying paints in a single layer and often completing a painting during a single session gave greater freedom of expression to the spontaneous painter.

A variety of materials have been used as painting supports, such as wooden panels, an assortment of paper substances, copper plates, glass, marble and slate. The wooden supports used by Flemish artists were generally made of pine sections that had been joined together and batoned on the reverse. The surface of the panel was prepared by sanding, sizing, and applying successive layers of thin gesso, a finely ground chalk mixed with size. Gesso proved too brittle to be used as a ground on the more flexible canvas supports, so it was replaced in the early part of the sixteenth century by white lead. The white, reflective gesso surface was polished to a high lustre, ready to receive tempera paint. The painter made his design on this surface with chalk or brush, usually working from preliminary drawings or colour renderings. An underpainting, in monochrome, was then established to unify the composition and create tonal contrasts between dark and light areas. Flesh tones were usually underpainted in green, the theory being that green bleeds through overlying flesh tones to neutralise and blend into a tonal half-shadow. Over the underpainting, colours were exactingly applied in a succession of minute, cross-hatched, or stippled brush strokes. The completed painting presented a lustrous and durable surface which would withstand the ravages of time admirably.

Tooling was an important feature of panel painting at this time. Pointed instruments, such as the stylus and compass, were used to incise lines in the gesso, and metal dies were used to create decorative patterns in the gold. Panels of religious subjects were partially painted gold and laid with gold leaf. Patterned gold leaf served as a rich embellishment which reflected the light of flickering candles in the dark recesses of the church. Sometimes beaten gold and silver ornaments or jewels in the forms of crowns, crests, swordhilts and scabbards were embedded in the paint itself.

Canvas was both scarce and expensive for quite some time after it first came into use. Today it is no longer scarce, but canvas of quality remains expensive. Linen used to be woven more narrowly than it is today, making it necessary to sew several widths together in order to prepare canvas for a large composition. The prepared canvas was either stretched and turned over the edges of a wooden stretcher frame or it was strung like a trampoline. The latter method is illustrated in several portraits of Flemish artists at work in their studios.

Vasari tells us that the Bellini family was typical of artists working in Venice at the time and that they preferred painting on canvas:

> Jacopo, with the assistance of his sons, painted the 'Miracle of the True Cross' for the Brotherhood of Saint John the Evangelist. This was done on canvas, as was customary in Venice, where they rarely use maple or poplar wood, as is usual elsewhere. In Venice they do not paint on panels or, if they do so occasionally, they then use only fir wood, imported from Germany or Slavonia. Canvas is the preferred material. Perhaps this is so because it does not split, does not suffer from worms, can be of any size, and is easily transported. Whatever the cause, the Bellini painted their first pictures on canvas.

In the past, much of our knowledge of the individual painting techniques of certain masters has been provided by their unfinished paintings. Prior to the use of X-ray and infra-red films, these paintings and written documentation were the only sources of information available about their working methods. The National Gallery in London is fortunate in having two unfinished paintings by Michelangelo.

THE PAINTER'S EQUIPMENT

Certain basic furniture and equipment were essential to a studio. The artist's easel would occupy the most suitable position to capture evenly distributed light. In one corner would stand a table which held the indispensable stone slab and muller for grinding raw colour pigments; beside the slab would be a mortar and pestle for crushing crude substances before they were ground. In close proximity to the easel there must be a cabinet for the storage of supplies. However, there is little evidence of this type of furniture being used extensively until the seventeenth century when it took the form of a compartmentalised box or small chest. In addition, there were various sundry necessities for the task of grinding colours, such as oils, varnishes, palette knives and bladders. The latter were used for storing prepared colours as there were no collapsible metal tubes manufactured until the late eighteenth or early nineteenth century; a fact which had confined artists to painting in the studio instead of out-of-doors.

The Old Masters' palettes were generally limited to approximately a dozen colours. Rubens' personal collection, apart from the earth colours, included madder, malachite, orpiment, ultramarine blue, vermilion, and vert azure. The artist was compelled to mix his colours carefully to obtain subtle variations and nuances.

Some pigments were obtained from earths, minerals and even semi-precious stones. The raw materials were ground and then bound into a painting medium by the addition of such substances as water, honey, egg or oil. Pigments from natural sources are either organic or inorganic. The organic pigments are composed of carbon and other elements and include madders, carmine, crimson lake, gamboge, indigo and various colours derived from coal or tar.

The inorganic colours include those derived from the combination of various substances with metals to form oxides and sulphides such as red and yellow ochre, genuine ultramarine blue, terre verte and vermilion.

Often, the raw materials had to be transported great distances to import dealers from whom the guilds selected quality materials and in turn sold them to the artists. Costly lapis lazuli, for example, was brought from the mountains of Afghanistan. It was considered indispensable for painting blue robes and materials in particular.

The gradual introduction of synthetically developed pigments in later centuries augmented those obtained from natural sources. Colour merchants today provide an endless range of hues and tints.

Few painters today keep the paraphernalia for preparing pigments that was once indispensable. Although pigments may be purchased for hand-grinding, artists more often prefer the convenience and uniformity of prepared oils. Picture restorers are a select group who still grind their own colours. By using hand-ground pigments, restorers are able to match more closely the coarseness of the pigment particles used by the Old Masters. Even the additives used to prepare pigments for painting, such as varnish, oils, driers and mediums, are analysed by conservation laboratories so that they may be made consistent with those used in the past.

An area of the studio was used for stretching canvas on to wooden frames and preparing panels. Pictures might be stored in the same corner, some completed and others drying or in various stages of progress, according to the artist's working habits. A stove or fireplace was necessary, especially in the Northern climes, to keep both the artist and his model warm.

In any studio the focus of attention is the easel which has certain basic requirements. It should be sufficiently stable to support a painting in a vertical position and must also accommodate canvases of varying dimensions. The artist should be able to raise or lower the picture and to tilt the angle of the easel in any direction necessary to prevent distracting reflections on the picture's surface. The tripod style easel depicted in the painting of Rembrandt's studio (plate p. 72) is typical of the age. Pegs could be inserted for adjusting the height of the painting, but a forward tilt was not possible.

A later development was the large studio easel with a crank winding apparatus to elevate the crossbar on which the painting rested. Instead of having three legs, the studio easel was mobile and constructed on a castor-wheeled base.

Portable outdoor painting easels were introduced in the nineteenth century. In recent times these portable kits have been cleverly designed to include compartments for the palette, paints, brushes and bottles as well as catches to secure a wet painting. The tripod legs are adjustable so that the painting can be kept level when working on the most uneven terrain. When the legs are folded, this transportable miniature studio can be carried like a valise or strapped on the back like a rucksack.

Small table-top easels have been constructed for the use of artists with limited floor space. They are also convenient for displaying paintings.

The palettes of the ancient Egyptians were made mainly of stone or bone. During the early Middle Ages palettes were small as the number of colours at the artist's disposal was still limited. Some were oval, while others were rectangular. Perhaps the earliest reference to the traditional paint-holder is a passage in the Mt Athos Manuscript, a painter's handbook of the eleventh century, which referred to a palette with a thumb-hole. In the days of the cathedral workshop the palette was often simply a board with a handle. In later centuries the size was increased to hold the new colours which had been added to an artist's repertoire.

Although wood has been the traditional material of artists' palettes throughout the history of easel painting, many other materials have been tried. Palettes of glass, porcelain, metal and synthetic materials have been in vogue while pads of disposable paper sheets have also been used.

In a workshop the painter would have the services of an apprentice to clean the used palette and prepare a fresh one with new pigments in an arrangement of the master's preference. The knives, or spatulas, used to scrape the palette were generally flat-bladed, semi-flexible metal. The modern and more pliable painting knives, which came into popular usage in the eighteenth century, have specially designed blades with rounded ends to aid in spreading paint.

Some form of fibrous tuft for carrying and manipulating paint has been in use since early man. Artists in ancient Egypt made brushes from reeds whose fibre ends were pounded and separated to a desired shape. Two principal types of brush have been employed by Western painters since the Middle Ages—those containing soft animal hair known as sable and those made of bristles, often referred to as hog. Before the early nineteenth century brushes were usually round in shape; the introduction of metal ferrule holders facilitated the making of flat brushes. Brushmaking was an activity generally carried out in the workshop until the seventeenth century when specialists in the craft began to supply them.

A mahlstick might be found in many studios from the sixteenth century onwards. This was a light stick a yard or more in length to which was affixed a soft leather-covered ball. The ball was placed against the easel or painting surface so that the painter could steady his hand while working on detailed areas. Several famous artists including Rembrandt have painted self-portraits with mahlsticks in hand.

By the nineteenth century a small box for transporting paints became a part of the artist's equipment. On occasion, Turner painted out-of-doors with oils using bladder bags for his pigments; however, most of his open-air scenes were painted in watercolour, since using oil paints was a tedious process. Constable carried a small paintbox on his journeys into the countryside. Many of his finest English landscape studies were painted on small panels using the open box lid as an easel.

Paper in small sheets or sketchbooks was kept in every studio. It was treated as a precious commodity and never wasted. Each sheet had to be made separately, but the slowness and care in the production of hand-made paper was also its strength, and its durability owes much to this.

Craftsmen engaged in making paper for books and documents also supplied artists' workshops. A few artists undertook the time-consuming process of papermaking with their own requirements in mind, occasionally toning the sheets in subtle shades with ink or watercolour.

Today, a vast range of art paper, mount board or academy board is available in a multitude of sizes or in continuous rolls. Unlike the hand-made papers, machine-made paper made from wood pulp and chemicals has a high acid content and is therefore subject to deterioration.

Reed and quill pens were preferred for drawing, although metal pens have been found dating from Roman times. The silver point was a popular instrument which the Old Masters used to great effect. When the silver point is drawn over a paper coated with a material of an abrasive character such as chalk or calcified bone, fine particles of silver are detached and appear as soft grey lines. It was not until the eighteenth century that the graphite pencil as we know it was introduced as a drawing instrument.

Charcoal for drawing on paper and for indicating preliminary lines on painting supports was a universal material dating from prehistoric times. Charcoal in stick form was prepared by roasting bundles of dry willow branches in an oven until they became black.

Pastels were prepared by combining paste with powdered pigments and water into which an adhesive such as gum arabic, soap or oatmeal might be added. Varying colour gradations were obtained by adding earth clays or Armenian bole for the darker colours. The paste substance was moulded and left to dry into small, cylindrical sticks. Hardness was achieved by adding wax.

In addition to the artist's equipment, the studios contained various items to be used as props for compositions. Landscapes might be composed by arranging a selection of small rocks and shrubs on a table. Still-life materials included table utensils, musical instruments, draperies and a variety of objects that the painter might find suitable for inclusion in his painting compositions.

ANATOMICAL AIDS

The studio of Rembrandt must surely have been one of the most interestingly furnished of the period. An inventory of the contents of his studio in 1656 lists many diverse objects used as subjects for his still lifes or as costuming and accessories for portraits and historical pageantry. In addition, there were many anatomical casts of Greek antique sculpture, plaster heads, arms, hands and faces individually moulded from which his pupils drew. Rembrandt was an avid collector and connoisseur of fine antiques and objects. In many self-portraits he is seen wearing or using some of his acquisitions. Rembrandt's expensive tastes were a prelude to his financial downfall. He could not resist spending the money he received for his paintings on his beloved *objets d'art* with complete disregard for his ebbing funds.

Mannikins, costumes and drapery were indispensable to painters of Biblical and historical occasions. The wooden mannikin, jointed to resemble a human body, remained the only reliable model for an artist who found it difficult to obtain the services of live ones willing to pose in the nude. If it was somewhat less satisfactory than a live model, the artist could at least console himself that a mannikin would not be late or grumble or, still more advantageous, would not require payment for services rendered. A larger and more elaborately constructed type of mannikin which was called a 'lay figure' was used by a number of painters during the nineteenth century.

The inspired artist's thirst for knowledge that would enrich his art led to the study of the anatomy of humans and animals. Michelangelo became an avid practitioner of anatomical dissection in his desire to discover the secrets of muscular structure. Among the later artist-anatomists was the English painter George Stubbs, famous for his superb anatomical drawings and paintings of equestrian subjects. A man of prodigious strength and conviction, Stubbs must have presented a spectacular sight as he grappled with the carcasses of the dead horses that he dragged up to his studio to be drawn and dissected.

Dissection of corpses in the Netherlands was unlawful until 1555 and after that time was permitted only on bodies of male criminals. In *Dutch and Flemish Painters*, Van Mander relates a story attributed to the Dutch painter Aert Mijtens which graphically illustrates the length to which an enthusiastic artist might go to make drawings or casts from life. In his eagerness to learn anatomy, Mijtens went to a nearby gallows to take down

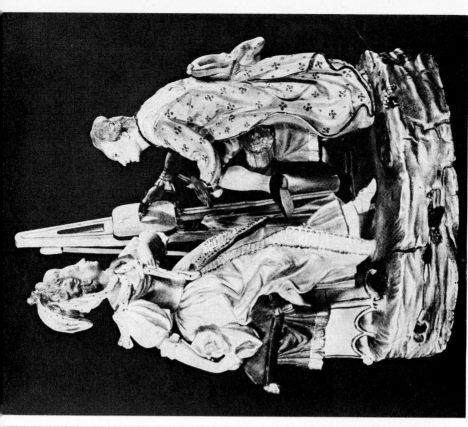

Page 71 (left) 'Lorenzo de'Medici' by Andrea del Verrocchio, *c* 1478, a life-size painted terracotta bust. *(right)* 'The Portrait Painter' by Antonio Grassi in Viennese porcelain, height 11¾in.; Grassi was a sculptor and the leading artist of the Royal Viennese Porcelain Factory in the eighteenth century

Page 72 (above) 'The Artist in His Studio' by Rembrandt; this unusual composition is thought to be a self-portrait. (below) 'An Artist in His Studio with Apprentices' by Stradanus; a fascinating display of the equipment and activities of a flourishing studio

Ioa. Stradanus invent.   Phls Galle excud.

the body of a criminal after his execution. He took with him an artist helper and a sack in which to carry back the corpse. After climbing the step ladder, he cut the rope that held the body, which slumped on to his assistant who was following him up the ladder. Unexpectedly receiving the weight of the corpse, the young man let out a terrifying cry and ran away as fast as his legs could carry him.

OPTICAL AND MECHANICAL DEVICES

The use of optical equipment in the studio began when these scientific instruments were in their infancy. Prior to that time, theories involving related fields of optical inventions and phenomena were under investigation by scientifically minded artists.

One of the numerous experiments Dürer employed in his study of perspective was an apparatus which consisted of an aperture through which threads were drawn from the object to the station point, materialising the visual rays into lines. The Italian Renaissance sculptor and architect, Brunelleschi, is considered by many to be the founder of modern perspective.

Perhaps the most graphic example of foreshortening of the supine figure occurs in Andrea Mantegna's painting 'The Dead Christ' in the Pinacoteca de Brera museum in Milan. The effect of the optical illusion that has been created in this picture is astonishing. If one stands near the painting, the torso of the dead Christ seems too large for the lower limbs. Retreating a few steps, one finds the figure has miraculously lengthened to correct proportions. Remarkably, if one moves to the right or left, the legs and body seem to move in an arc with the viewer's line of vision, so that the feet are always pointing directly towards the viewer.

Mirror images, particularly for self-portraits, had a widespread fascination for artists in the later Middle Ages. The masterpiece 'Las Meninas' (plate p. 89) by Velasquez depicts the painter studying the reflected images of himself and members of the royal family and court in a large mirror and admirably illustrates the painter's preoccupation with the multiple spatial planes possible. Flemish artists such as Jan van Eyck, Quentin Massys and Petrus Christus painted images reflected in a convex mirror. Van Eyck's elaborately framed convex mirror in his famous painting 'The Marriage of Arnolfini' reflects the entire room in miniature. In his splendid work 'The Ambassadors' Holbein painted a skull distorted

5

by mirror reflection which is thought by some to be a symbol of his name, Holbein, meaning skull in German.

The artist's apparent obsession for optics reached its ultimate form in the *trompe l'oeil* constructions of the Dutch painter Hoogstraten one of which is now displayed in London's National Gallery. These specially designed illuminated boxes have peepholes for viewing the interiors of what appear to be completely furnished rooms, but are, in reality, flat surfaces cleverly painted in illusory third dimension.

One of the earliest and most promising of the optical instruments was the camera obscura. This device consists of a darkened chamber in which an image of an object is received through a small opening or lens focused in natural colour on to a facing paper surface for tracing. The camera obscura may be small enough to be contained in a hand-held box or large enough for a man to enter like a chamber. Illustrations exist of portable camera obscuras for working outdoors which were carried like sedan chairs supported on poles. It has been suggested that Vermeer may have employed a camera obscura because of certain illusionary optical devices in his paintings. If so, Vermeer most probably used it to heighten a sense of realism.

The camera obscura was used by several important artists from the sixteenth century onwards, but it was in the eighteenth century that it became widely and systematically employed. The Italian *veduta* painters, Canaletto, Guardi and Bellotto, certainly made use of this instrument as it suited architectural and topographical subjects admirably. It was, however, necessary for the artist to have a sound knowledge of perspective in order to correct the distortions which would appear in panoramic scenes.

A similar device, the camera lucida, is a more sophisticated optical instrument that incorporates a prism to deflect light rays from an object on to paper for tracing. It was sold by artists' suppliers from 1850 but it was invented and used at a considerably earlier date.

An instrument which achieved popularity during the seventeenth and eighteenth centuries was the Claude Lorraine Glass, named after the painter who developed and used it. The apparatus utilised a small black convex mirror which reflected low-key images of supposedly Claudian character, enabling sketches and drawings to be made from reflections observed in the glass. This provided both artists and tourists with picturesque impressions.

The graphic telescope, patented in England in 1811 by Cornelius Varley, was a further development of the camera obscura and the camera lucida. John Sell Cotman is known to have used the graphic telescope while painting in the open.

All the optical aids mentioned were superseded by the invention of the camera. The oft-quoted remark by painter Paul Delaroche, upon learning of Daguerre's discovery, 'From today painting is dead' has not proved to be true. The photograph cannot replace the painting, but it has had a remarkable influence upon the concept of what painting might be. The camera records every detail in a scene, but the artist is free to transpose this information, rearranging, adding or deleting pictorial elements as he chooses. Sometimes the camera can provide quite new information, as when Eadweard Muybridge's photographs of galloping horses showed that the positions of their legs at any given moment were different from the poses that artists had traditionally imagined and depicted.

Mechanical instruments, such as the pantograph and other similar devices, were used for making enlarged or reduced copies by direct tracing. The pantograph consists of two individual styluses for tracing and copying. These are set into four rods with movable joints in the form of a parallelogram with extended sides. The pantograph is said to have been in use since the early nineteenth century.

The artist's interest in new devices for tracing, enlarging or perspective has been recorded in paintings and drawings. Many painters have depicted themselves utilising these aids in self-portraits, allowing us an intimate glimpse into their surroundings, equipment and working habits. 'The Painter's Studio' by Vermeer, reproduced on the dust jacket, showing the artist working on a canvas with a toned ground, graphically records his technique for art historians. The plumes of the model's headdress are painted in detail on the grey-toned canvas, suggesting that he may have painted his compositions piecemeal. Unlike his contemporaries he apparently painted directly on the support without any underpainting.

CHAPTER 6

STUDIO MASTERS

The most renowned art workshops of Europe were concentrated in the North (the Netherlands, Flanders and Germany) or in the South (Italy and, to a lesser extent, France). Italian artists almost completely dominated the eleventh, twelfth and thirteenth centuries. During the Renaissance some of their *bottegas* (workshops) became centres for philosophical thought on the arts and teaching in addition to producing works of art. By the sixteenth century northern artists were strongly established with guild workshops which for more than a century nourished many of the great masters we still admire today. From early medieval times nearly every painter was taught by a master in a workshop and in turn became a master himself. It is not practical to list here all the artists who established workshops, as this was customary practice for especially gifted painters. Occasionally painters of lesser distinction became masters, but because of the repetitious and uninspired quality of their work they were often referred to as masters of 'art factories' where assembly-line techniques were employed.

In most instances the success of large workshops was directly linked to the master's own talents and initiative. The contribution to the art world of a few masters of lesser stature was to have discovered or taught those who are acknowledged today as great artists. A few outstanding examples of Northern and Southern masters who typify both are presented here.

A SHOPKEEPING MASTER

Francesco Squarcione (*c*1394–*c*1474) remains one of the most remarkable and enigmatic figures of art history. He was past forty when he gave up his business as a tailor and embroiderer in Padua to open a painting work-shop. Until this time he had had little acquaintance with the art profession, other than travelling to Rome and Greece to purchase works of classic sculpture which he displayed and sold in his shop. Gradually, as he amassed a larger collection of antiquities, artists called on him to ask permission to make drawings of the statues. The studio became a meeting-place for painting and the discussion of archaeology and art. Quick to assess and utilise talent, he persuaded a number of artists and apprentices to work for him in fulfilling commissions from clients.

Rather than a master, Squarcione might more accurately be described as the entrepreneur of a thriving art business. Although only two mediocre paintings can be attributed to his own hand, Squarcione nevertheless succeeded in qualifying for admission to the Guild of Painters in Padua in 1441. In the same year he adopted a young nameless orphan of ten years of age as his son and pupil. This talented youth became known as the illustrious Andrea Mantegna. It was the increasing fame of Mantegna that brought young artists flocking to the studio in Padua.

Fortune again bestowed its blessings on Squarcione with the arrival in Padua of the celebrated Venetian painter, Jacopo Bellini. Utilising his per-suasive powers, he soon enlisted Bellini into his business as both painter and teacher. There is little doubt that it was Bellini's genius which inspired the students in general and young Mantegna in particular.

Eventually Bellini tired of his secondary role to the less talented Squarcione and left the firm to establish a rival studio. Mantegna, with his reputation already established, followed suit; he opened his own workshop in Padua and married the daughter of Jacopo Bellini. Squarcione never for-gave Mantegna for what he considered to be the ultimate act of disloyalty.

At the height of his studio's success, Francesco Squarcione was the master of 137 pupils, many of whom acquired fame and followers. He was responsible for the founding of new schools of painting in Venice, Bologna, Ferrara, Lombardy and Parma. These important contributions to art his-tory came from a man whose own artistic talent was seemingly insignificant.

A MASTER SURPASSED

Andrea del Verrocchio (1435–1488) was the outstanding Florentine sculp-tor in the latter part of the fifteenth century. Records of his early training are somewhat shadowy and do not indicate the name of his first master, but it has been suggested that he was taught by Donatello. He was enrolled in the goldsmiths' guild in about 1457 and in the sculptors' guild in 1469. It was not until 1472 that he became a member of the Painters' Company of St Luke, during which time he was an assistant in a large *bottega*.

In the 1480s Verrocchio moved into the former studio of Donatello where he established a large and prosperous shop. The sound of chisels ringing on marble was echoed by a flood of commissions, making it the most active and renowned *bottega* in Florence. The Medici, his most important patrons, conferred an honour upon Verrocchio by appointing him master of the family tomb. A prolific worker, Verrocchio undertook every type of commission within the artistic sphere. Lorenzo di Credi, Verrocchio's chief assistant, was able to finish only a small portion of the huge volume of work his master had contracted before his death.

Verrocchio's studio became the training-ground for the most gifted Italian artists of the time. The sculptors who were in attendance included Benedetto Buglioni and Giovanni Francesco Rustici. Verrocchio trained many painters, several of whom achieved great fame, including Leonardo da Vinci, Luca Signorelli, Domenico Ghirlandaio, Pietro Perugino and the inheritor of his artistic legacy, Lorenzo di Credi.

Beyond doubt the most important pupil in his shop was Leonardo da Vinci who as a painter over-shadowed his master almost from the start. The eclectic nature of the studio made a vivid impression on Leonardo, whose inherent genius and sensitivity permitted him to surpass his master in most artistic skills. Verrocchio instilled in him an appreciation of the designs of nature which might be found in the swirls and undulations of sea currents or the woven rhythms of a woman's hair. Not all the influences of the young Leonardo stemmed from his master; he assimilated the style of another flourishing Florentine studio run by the brothers Antonio and Piero del Pollaiuolo as well.

Leonardo is supposed to have painted an angel in one of the most important paintings attributed to Verrocchio, the 'Baptism of Christ' in the Uffizi Gallery, Florence. A story by Vasari concerning this painting perpetuates the legend of the marvellous talent of Leonardo:

> Andrea Verrocchio never stopped working; he was always painting or doing sculpture, changing from one to another. A picture for the nuns of San Domenico was such a success that he painted another for the monks of Vallombrosa. The subject was the Baptism of Christ. Leonardo painted one of the angels. It was obvious that this was the best part of the picture, and Andrea resolved never to paint again because he had been outdone by one so young.

Although there may be some truth in the story, it is more likely that the endless administrative duties of his studio had a greater bearing on Verrocchio's subsequent lack of interest in painting; thereafter he concentrated on sculpture and goldsmithing. The quality of his sculpture places him in the front rank alongside the truly great masters of the Renaissance.

Verrocchio was the epitome of the eclectic Renaissance man, at least within the applied arts. He was at the same time a painter of considerable merit and an accomplished designer of costumes and banners, as well as an experienced goldsmith and jeweller. Above all, he excelled in the plastic arts—clay modelling and sculpting in marble and bronze. He was also noted as a teacher of considerable knowledge and influence. Verrocchio did much to project a new image of the artist's role in society and to impress upon the public the dignity of art as a vocation.

A GERMAN ART FACTORY

Lucas Sunder, or Maler, was the real name of the celebrated German artist Lucas Cranach (1472–1553) who later took this name to identify with his native town Kronach in Bavaria. This was merely the first step in the artist's plan to impress his name upon the good citizens of Franconia.

Little is known of Cranach's early years other than that he trained in the engraving studio of his father Hans until 1498. At the turn of the century he was in Vienna, where he became famous for his excellent portraits. By 1504 he had made his reputation and was invited to Wittenberg to become Court Painter to Prince Frederick the Wise. It was in Wittenberg that Cranach established his workshop and became burgomaster of the town. He successively painted for John the Steadfast and John Frederick the Magnanimous. Their likenesses were at first painted by Cranach and then repeated scores of times by the members of his workshop. In 1508 he was granted an armorial crest of a winged dragon; it remained the signature for the prodigious output of the studio even after his death.

Cranach embraced the German Reformation with considerable fervour. He was a close friend of Martin Luther and executed several fine portraits of the monk which still exist. Cranach was a contemporary of Raphael and Michelangelo, but his influences were utterly Germanic, stemming mainly from Dürer. This is particularly evident in his woodcuts which were important money-spinners for the studio. He made many hundreds of prints using his drawings as a basis for engravings. The portraits of the great Reformers were extremely popular and became widely circulated.

Cranach's commercial undertakings and intellectual ability were instrumental in achieving wealth and social success during his career. Today his fame rests largely upon his creation of a personal style in painting sensual female nudes with elongated limbs, high-set breasts and narrow hips, quite in opposition to the more rotund or unflatteringly realistic figures of other painters. Their titles were chosen from historical or mythological subjects for the sake of the puritanical propriety of the times. Under the guise of Venus, Diana or Bathsheba, smooth-skinned flaxen-haired maidens, sometimes elegantly coiffeured, made Cranach as famous for his nudes as Raphael was for his madonnas. The use of transparent drapery in these paintings only served to heighten their sensuality and eroticism.

Some criticism of Lucas Cranach resulted because, in his commercial zeal, he often undertook enterprises unworthy of his talents. As an industrious artist with limited time, he frequently applied to his picture-making formula assembly-line techniques. He prepared the designs and directed the work, but his assistants and pupils were charged with the actual execution of the majority of the paintings that were issued from his shop.

Although the reputation of most so-called art factories suffered as a result of the mediocrity of the work they produced, Cranach's studio maintained a surprisingly high quality of production. A certain amount of unevenness in the paintings can generally be attributed to the master's brushwork, which was superior to that of any of his assistants.

Cranach delegated considerable authority to his sons Lucas and Hans, who in turn supervised ten assistants. Lucas the younger, the most devoted of his sons, kept the studio in high gear and perpetuated his father's style; the son's death marked the end of a continuous span of eighty years' production by this famous studio.

Cranach died in Weimar, Germany, where his house may still be seen. More than a thousand paintings from the workshop have survived.

RAPHAEL, THE SOUTHERN MASTER

Raffaello Sanzio, painter and architect, was appropriately named after the archangel Raphael. He was born at Urbino in 1483, the son of Giovanni Santi, an undistinguished painter who gave Raphael his first instruction in art. He died in Rome in 1520 at the age of thirty-seven.

Perhaps no other artist in history has been accorded such rapturous eulogistic praise as the sublime genius, Raphael Sanzio of Urbino. Raphael has been described by countless writers as handsome in person and charming in manner and conversation. He captivated all whom he met, save those malicious persons who wished to rival him but could not.

Raphael's fame survived the passage of time and he remained one of the principal influences on young painters until the present century. He was the exalted and enshrined ideal of every painter for his artistic purity. Sadly, Raphael's style is no longer in vogue.

Little is known of his early years, but undoubtedly he was a youthful prodigy and probably entered the studio of Timoteo Vitti as a pupil. By 1499, at the age of sixteen, he was at work in the shop of Perugino where he assisted in painting frescoes for the hall at *Colegio del Cambio* in Perugia. It is probable that he accompanied the master on his frequent journeys to Florence. Raphael assimilated Perugino's style so completely that, according to Vasari, 'his copies cannot be distinguished from the original works!' It was Raphael's inherent genius that enabled him to evolve his own style and prevented him from becoming merely another slavish follower of this master.

By the beginning of 1505 Raphael had moved to Florence to begin an intensive study of Florentine art. He absorbed the atmosphere of this city where the great masters Michelangelo and Leonardo da Vinci were at work. Raphael was a youth of twenty-five at the time, while Michelangelo was thirty and Leonardo fifty-three; yet he was soon to rival these masters in this decade which heralded the High Renaissance.

From the earlier inspiration of Donatello, Antonio Pollaiuolo and Fra Bartolommeo, he made copies and studies of various compositions. His interpretations seem to be more evocations of the spirit of the artists than tedious facsimiles of their work. Knowledge of his talent spread and he was given many important commissions for the churches of Florence. A few of these paintings showed promise of the genius that was soon to flower.

Towards the end of 1508 Raphael went to Rome and was introduced to the papal court by his mentor Bramante who was the chief architect of the papal palaces. In 1509 Pope Julius II was having his apartments decorated by a group of artists that included Lotto, Sodoma and Bramantino. However, after seeing samples of Raphael's work, the Pope was so impressed that he dismissed the others and gave his new favourite free rein in the completion of the decorations.

These rooms in the Vatican were known collectively as the *Stanze*. The first one Raphael decorated was called the *Stanza della Segnatura* because it was there that the ecclesiastical tribunal of the Segnatura met. The paintings in this room depict the reconciliation of philosophy and astrology with theology. They were inspired by the ideals of ancient Rome, just as, in his madonnas, Raphael sought to emulate classical Greek sculpture.

The paintings of the second room are of dramatic Biblical themes such as 'Heliodorus Driven Out of the Temple at Jerusalem'. In the third room the principal work, 'The Fire in the Borgo', is almost entirely by Raphael's own hand. The fourth room was painted by his assistants; it contains the 'Battle of Constantine' and was the last of the decorative schemes in the Vatican apartments.

During the time Raphael was occupied with the Vatican commission, Michelangelo was painting his glorious cycle in the Sistine Chapel. The unveiling of this monumental work took place in 1512. Many students of art history have concluded that the excitement engendered by the magnificence of the Sistine ceiling led Raphael to attempt to create a more dramatic effect in the second *Stanza*.

The fame of this son of Urbino had spread across the civilised Western world. Much of this fame was due to publicity provided by the remarkably talented Marcantonio Raimondi, whose brilliant engravings after Raphael's paintings reached every major *atelier* in Western Europe.

In the period from 1509 to 1520 Raphael executed many commissions for Popes Julius II and Leo X. During this time he continued to paint numerous easel pictures, frescoes and altarpieces in his increasingly busy studio. His eloquence and talent secured him a place of favour when Leo X was elevated to the pontifical throne. Leo X, a humanist and patron of the arts, surrounded himself with men of letters who similarly aspired to create a cultural revival in Rome.

Raphael's work on the *Stanze* had revealed his genius as a great historical painter as well as a creator of beautiful madonnas. Moreover, his accomplishments in the field of architectural design led to his appointment as Chief Architect of St Peter's and Surveyor and Guardian of the Ancient Monuments of Rome. In addition to assuming this position, he acted in a similar capacity as architect for the banker Agostino Chigo for whom he designed stage scenery for the theatre.

In 1515–16, Raphael undertook one of his most important commissions —the design of ten cartoons for tapestries which were to decorate the lower walls of the Sistine Chapel. These tapestries are still in the Vatican. Seven of the original cartoons, which were almost entirely by Raphael's own hand, are in the Victoria and Albert Museum, London, on loan from the Royal Collection.

During this period he also supervised the painting of a fresco series based on subjects from the Old Testament for the Loggia of the Vatican. His desire for accuracy was so great that he employed agents as far afield as Greece to search for pertinent material on this theme.

Clients continued unceasingly to commission paintings of madonnas and the Holy Family. Although Raphael drew preliminary studies for painting compositions and tapestry cartoons, the execution of the majority of these commissions was left in the hands of his numerous assistants. He always took care to supervise the design and completion of every work and, when necessary, to improve upon certain passages with his brush; many of these paintings purported to be entirely by his own hand and bore his signature.

The volume of commissions soon became overwhelming and Raphael was forced to procrastinate—promising a delivery date that he was unable to meet, then making excuses for the delay. In order to fulfil these many commitments, it was necessary to employ more assistants and the studio hummed with activity. At one time there were more than fifty artists at work. Every conceivable variety of art was produced, including paintings, engravings, enamelling and mosaics. It was not difficult to find pupils or talented painters since Raphael's fame as a gifted master was widespread. In a few instances he engaged the services of specialist painters such as Giovanni da Udine, who painted beautiful festoons of flowers and fruit, to collaborate with him on certain commissions.

Several paintings of the Holy Family that were executed during Raphael's last years are undoubtedly from his designs, but they were painted by his two chief assistants, Giulio Romano and Giovan Francesco Penni, whose styles echoed that of their master. Similarly, these two reliable artists are believed by many scholars to have painted the frescoes of the third *Stanza* in a style following Raphael's compositional designs.

In addition to his painting *bottega*, he was also in charge of a workshop of architectural assistants who undertook the supervision of constructions. To his architectural stable he was able to summon the talented Sangallo family as collaborators. Giuliano da Sangallo had been assistant to the architect of St Peter's. Antonio da Sangallo remained with the workshop until Raphael's death; he is given considerable credit as collaborator on the work of St Peter's.

Though his lifespan was short, the volume of work Raphael produced in the space of a few years can be attributed to his prodigious efforts and to the fact that he maintained an enormous workshop of assistants. Michelangelo and Leonardo preferred to create fewer works but ones which they personally executed.

In 1520 Raphael died suddenly after several days of fever. His lying in state was attended by the highest personages in the land; his last work, the 'Transfiguration', commissioned by Cardinal Giulio de' Medici (later Pope Clement VIII), was displayed at his head.

In his will Raphael bequeathed the remaining works in his studio to his faithful assistants Romano and Penni with instructions for them to finish all the commissions still on hand. He left a fortune of 16,000 florins and several properties.

The imprint Raphael made on art history was considerable. He worked industriously and achieved glorious fame through his large workshop production. Caravaggio was most certainly influenced by Raphael while others such as Guido Reni, Poussin and the Carraccis borrowed freely from him. For four centuries thereafter, artists looked back to Raphael for inspiration.

RUBENS, THE NORTHERN MASTER

Peter Paul Rubens was born in Antwerp in 1577, the son of an advocate and alderman. He received a sound classical education and began to draw and paint on his own initiative, eventually becoming apprenticed at the age of thirteen to the landscape painter Tobias Verhaecht. His tasks befitted a young apprentice; he was permitted to grind colours, wash brushes and tidy the studio. His most important training began when he was allowed to observe the master at work and to copy his paintings.

After a short period of study with Verhaecht, Rubens left to enter the studio of another Antwerp artist, Adam van Noort, who specialised in painting figure compositions. Rubens spent four profitable years under van Noort's tutelage. According to the records of the Guild of St Luke, Rubens was elected to the title of Master of the Guild in 1598. At the age of twenty-one he left to work for a short period in the studio of Otto van Veen, an artist who, like many of his northern contemporaries, was inspired by the Italian masters.

Following those early formative years, Rubens journeyed to Italy in 1600 to steep himself in the atmosphere of the country that had produced Leonardo, Michelangelo and Raphael. The maturation of his character and technique was greatly influenced by the eight years he spent in the heady atmosphere of the great Italian art centres.

In Venice, where artists were creating works unparalleled in the world, Rubens chanced to meet an emissary of the Duke of Gonzaga, who recognised Rubens' potential and introduced his work to the duke, who invited the young artist into his service in Mantua. The Gonzaga family had a tradition of fine-art patronage and owned works by Mantegna, Correggio, Titian and Raphael. It was in the palatial house of Gonzaga that Rubens found the arcadian surroundings which delighted him and helped formulate his cultured tastes. The duke was also instrumental in arranging Rubens' travels to Rome for the purpose of undertaking other commissions.

Rubens had arrived in Italy at a time when creative artistic forces were near their apex. The magnificent decoration of churches and palaces adorned with sculpture, gilding, ornate altarpieces and retables was complemented by public buildings and private homes embellished with paintings and frescoes on ceilings and walls. These subjects alluded to the highest aspirations of man and the glorification of God. Biblical scenes, allegories, fables and portraits were the subject-matter to which the artist applied himself, often with both religious and commercial zeal.

Rubens was summoned home because of the illness of his mother; he laid plans for the establishment of a studio in Antwerp before leaving Italy. His travels and work in Italy and later in Spain made a profound impression upon him that was to be a dominating influence for the rest of his life.

In 1609, the year following his departure from Italy, Rubens was appointed Court Painter to the Archduke Albert and Archduchess Isabella. In the same year he married Isabella Brandt who became the model for several of his paintings. After her death several years later, he married Hélène Fourment who also served as an inspiring model.

The age of the workshop as a centre for productive artistic talent was at its height in the seventeenth century. Active as many of the workshops were, none could be said to have achieved the degree of legendary fame that has been accorded the studio of Peter Paul Rubens.

Rubens established his studio in the courtyard of his Antwerp home. The exterior of the studio was decorated ornately in the Italian manner with a baroque triumphal arch adjoining the garden. In 1937 the studio became the property of the city of Antwerp and was restored to its original state (plate p. 125). To cope with the increasing number of new commissions, a large retinue of assistants and pupils was engaged in his studio. Pupils flocked to him, as evidenced by a letter written to Monsieur de Bie by Rubens two years after his return from Italy:

> I am very glad to see that you place such confidence in me that you ask me to render you a service, but I regret from the bottom of my heart that I have no opportunity to show you by deeds rather than by words my regard for you. For it is impossible for me to accept the young man

whom you recommend. From all sides applications reach me. Some young men remain here for several years with other masters, awaiting a vacancy in my studio. Among others, my friend and (as you know) patron, Mr. Rockox, has only with great difficulty obtained a place for a youth whom he himself brought up, and whom, in the meantime, he was having trained by others. I can tell you truly, without any exaggeration, that I have refused over one hundred, even some of my own relatives or my wife's, and not without causing great displeasure among many of my best friends.

Not all of the work of the studio was completed by Rubens or his assistants. On many occasions he collaborated with fellow artists who specialised in painting particular subjects with consummate skill. A painting of an outdoor bacchanalian scene might, for example, be composed of a landscape painted by Jan Wildens, or still life and flower garlands might be undertaken by Jan Bruegel in a composition where the dominant figure subjects were left for Rubens' masterful brush strokes.

Jan Bruegel, nicknamed 'Velvet Bruegel', presumably because of his penchant for velvet material, was the most talented descendant of the great artist Pieter Bruegel the Elder and excelled in painting flowers, landscape and animals. The skill and unique sensitivity of Rubens and Bruegel complemented each other's work.

Jan Wildens sojourned five years in Italy and was an accomplished painter before he came to Rubens. He and the copyist/etcher Lucas van Uden were responsible for the inventive and skilfully composed landscape backgrounds of many pictures executed in Rubens' workshop.

Another collaborator and fellow master was Jacob Jordaens, whose early life had been similar to that of Rubens. He was born in Antwerp and became apprenticed to the studio of van Noort where he remained for eight years. He married van Noort's daughter and was admitted to the guild in 1616 as a watercolour painter. By 1621 he was head of both the guild and his own thriving workshop. He is best known for his genre paintings depicting riotous banquet scenes and coarse Flemish life. Although he was technically gifted, his choice of rather banal subject matter and apparent lack of divine inspiration precluded his achieving a fame comparable to that of Van Dyck or Rubens.

Frans Snyders had been a pupil of Pieter Bruegel the Younger and of Hendrick van Balen. He was a superlative painter of animals and still life and produced several superb hunting scenes of his own. Although Snyders also collaborated with Jordaens on several occasions, he became one of the chief assistants to Rubens.

None of these painters achieved a fame as great as that of the young Anthony van Dyck who was undoubtedly the most talented artist in Rubens' studio. His virtuosity was such that Rubens let him work upon areas of pictures which he usually reserved for himself. During the period of the great studios, genius was recognised and rewarded, and admiration for the skills of another was seldom prejudiced by rivalry. The good reputation of the studio and all concerned therein was the primary objective.

Van Dyck was born in 1599 in Antwerp, the city that spawned many of the great painters of the sixteenth and seventeenth centuries. Like Snyders, he studied with van Balen and had already established his reputation when he entered the Rubens' workshop. At that time his style tended to exaggerate that of Rubens, although coarser and muddier in tone, but with a decisive flair for the treatment of light. It was a happy relationship for both artists, but Van Dyck, with his great potential and ambition, could not be content for ever working in the shadow of a famous master. So Rubens bade farewell to his favourite assistant and they parted amicably.

Rubens took the ultimate responsibility for all work produced in the studio no matter how small his personal contribution may have been. In letters to patrons he made quite candid revelations concerning the practice of using assistants and pupils to work on his paintings. A declaration from his studio might describe a painting to be 'Original by my Hand except a most beautiful landscape, done by the hand of a master skilful in that department'. He would refer to copies of pictures made by his pupils as 'So well retouched by my hand that they are hardly to be distinguished from the originals'. Rubens took into consideration the degree of his own participation in a work when determining the scale of prices charged for paintings; thus works that were entirely by his own hand commanded the greatest sums.

In addition to his forthright attitude concerning the degree of his assistants' participation in the completion of works, Rubens was also quite content to allow other artists to retouch his work. In one instance, suspecting that the flesh tones in one of his paintings had become yellow through a long period of transit and storage, he wrote to a colleague:

But since you are such a great man in our profession, you will easily remedy this by exposing it to the sun, and leaving it there at intervals. And if need be, you may, with my permission, put your hand to it and retouch it wherever damage or my carelessness may render it necessary.

Three centuries later another illustrious hand was to make additions to a

Rubens painting, although Rubens might not have approved the alteration. This unauthorised retouching was carried out by Sir Winston Churchill at Chequers during World War II. The painting that received his attention was Rubens' 'Lion and the Mouse', based on the Aesop fable of the mouse freeing the lion. Unable to satisfactorily distinguish the mouse, Sir Winston took up his brush and made it more prominent.

Rubens, with the aid of his staff, was one of the most famous and prolific copyists. Copies were made of pictures by many of the great Renaissance artists such as Leonardo, Titian and Raphael.

Time was the most important factor in Rubens' personal productivity. While he could delegate much of the actual painting to his staff, the burden of administration was entirely his. In addition to supervising the daily activities of the studio, he had to confer with patrons concerning the many details of commissions and schedules for completion of work. He engaged in a volume of correspondence with patrons and clients in distant lands. His duties also included collaborating with the guild in matters of mutual interest such as the entertainment of visiting patrons, artists and dignitaries.

Rubens' painting time was further reduced by his involvement in affairs of state. His flair for politics and diplomacy was perceived and utilised by those in positions of influence, and he was sent on important missions to convey secret information directly to the rulers of Spain and England. These journeys served to increase his prestige in the dual roles of painter and diplomat. In England, he received the degree of Master of Arts at Cambridge and was knighted by Charles I in 1630; the following year he received a knighthood from Philip IV of Spain.

It would not have been possible for Rubens to have painted the large number of works that he did in his lifetime had he been a slow, methodical worker; he was charged with great energy which manifested itself in speed of execution and power of concentration. When Rubens was at his easel, the eyes of his pupils and assistants frequently strayed from their tasks to observe the master at work.

The studio served to focus all of Rubens' unique artistic talents. The earlier eclecticism in works influenced by Italian masters evolved into his own inventive style. This style was characterised by clarity of light and boldness of subject that made paintings by other artists appear static by comparison.

Rubens filled his canvases with a galaxy of gods and goddesses, wood nymphs and sartyrs engaged in bacchanalian orgies. Sumptuous banqueting scenes, huntresses with ample bosoms and voluptuous hips are con-

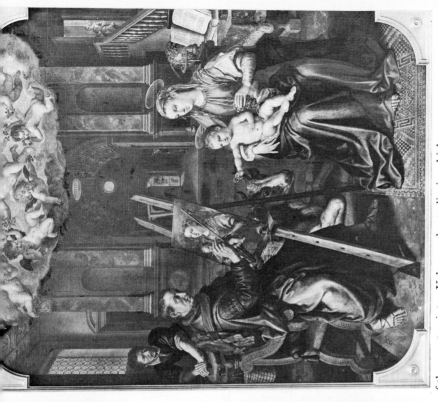

Page 89 (left) 'Las Meninas' by Velasquez. The interior of the court painter Velasquez's studio in which he depicts himself at work on a painting of the king and queen. The viewer should imagine that he is standing in the place of the royal couple who are seen reflected in the mirror, and viewing this scene as we see it, with Velasquez standing beside their daughter the Infanta Margarita and her entourage of maids of honour (*meninas*), tutors and dwarfs. (*right*) 'St Luke Painting the Virgin' by Marten de Vos. A whimsical composition showing St Luke resting his wrist on a mahlstick while painting a detailed passage; in the background an assistant grinds colours on a stone slab

Page 90 (above) 'Draughtsman Drawing a Portrait' by Albrecht Dürer, a woodcut made in 1525 from Dürer's treatise on perspective. The artist sights his seated model through a framed glass and paints what he sees, thus translating a three-dimensional subject to a two-dimensional surface. *(below)* Two more illustrations from Dürer's treatise on perspective

trasted by Biblical subjects in other paintings. Seldom have the sacred and the profane been treated with such devotion by the same artist. His abduction and battle scenes of this period are fluidly executed in a twisting juxtaposition of men, women and horses—their undulating bodies and flowing garments vibrant with colour. His nudes possess a sensuousness and lusty vigour quite unlike those of his contemporaries. He dispensed with any allegorical pretence in the realistic depiction of 'Hélène Fourment in a Fur Coat' (plate p. 108). The essence of Rubens' sensual nature is exemplified by the delight with which he rendered paint into pulsating flesh, painted so lifelike that, as Renoir said, 'you could pinch their bottoms'. Artists still describe a female model of ample proportions as having 'a figure like a Rubens'.

Rubens' method of painting nudes was to underpaint his canvas in transparent brown and white on a white priming. Over this he added flesh colours which were rendered thin in shadow areas, allowing the under-modelling to bleed through and create the pearly grey tones for which he is famous. He built up nuances of warm flesh tones against cool backgrounds, adding impasto highlights. Rubens painted rapidly in an inspired manner. Figures came to life with paint miraculously transformed to vibrant pink and glowing flesh. The pure joy of the act of painting springs forth from his canvases and his spontaneity may be appreciated by the viewer centuries later. Spontaneity of technique should not imply that Rubens painted in a haphazard manner; he worked under perfect control, confident of achieving his intended goal. Much of this control was the result of the elaborate preparations he made before painting the final composition.

Rubens made small-scale preliminary renderings of most of his paintings as a guide for his assistants. These were often done on white-primed wooden panels, seldom larger than three by four feet. Sometimes he used his brush as a drawing instrument, accentuating lines in sepia here and there to build the picture. His brush never hesitated; he painted with an intuitive rhythm consistent with an assured conviction of the ultimate perfection of the painting. These preliminary paintings, though devoid of detail, contained all the elements essential to the final composition. In some instances they have a freshness of spirit and handling that is somewhat lacking in the final version—a lack that is most evident in pictures painted by his pupils.

The publication of engravings and woodcuts that were made after paintings was a practice that proved quite valuable in spreading the fame of a workshop. Those produced in Rubens' studio were so popular that he was

6

compelled to copyright his designs to prevent other engravers from imitating them. Copyrights were generally of short duration and were not easily obtained. Dürer was plagued by a host of imitators in his lifetime and their copies were contested in court.

Eventually Rubens employed the talented Lucas Vorsterman as his chief engraver. His previous engraver, Pieter Soutman, had proved to be quite clever technically but failed to satisfy Rubens. Vorsterman was a gifted young engraver who worked industriously and profitably for Rubens over a number of years until, suffering from megalomania, he became convinced that he was not receiving enough public adulation for his works. Rubens wrote in 1622:

> Unfortunately we have made almost nothing for a couple of years, due to the caprices of my engraver who had to let himself sink into a dead calm, so that I can no longer deal with him or come to an understanding with him. He contends that it is his engraving alone and his illustrious name that give these prints any value.

In 1611 the Guild of Arquebusiers asked Rubens to paint an altarpiece, the 'Descent from the Cross', for the guild's chapel in the Church of Notre Dame in Antwerp. His friend and patron, Nicolaas Rockox, chief of the guild, was responsible for Rubens' receiving this first important commission. The powerful painting won him further acclaim and new patrons.

The artist could not always expect payment in cash for his work. There were those among the hierarchy of the state and church who sought to obtain or commission works on the basis that their patronage in itself was sufficient compensation in that it accorded publicity for the artist.

A master who had 'arrived' was less likely to be subjected to this kind of chicanery and certainly Rubens had become established by that time. Indeed, emissaries and agents from many influential quarters vied for his services. Yet there was always a capricious client who, by virtue of his wealth and influence, was recognised as a valuable asset to the prosperity of the studio, and who might attempt to barter rather than pay cash for his commissions. Such a man was Sir Dudley Carleton, an English diplomat and an avid collector.

To be fair, it was Rubens who instigated the bartering by writing to Sir Dudley, then serving as English Ambassador at The Hague. Rubens stated that he was willing to exchange some of his paintings for some ancient marble statues Sir Dudley had collected while serving in Italy. Rubens, like many other cultured artists of the time, was a keen collector, intent upon decorating his villa in Antwerp with works of antiquity and other sumptuous furnishings.

Sir Dudley Carleton was a dealer as well as a collector and most of his purchases had proved profitable. On one occasion Sir Dudley instigated correspondence with Rubens urging him to accept a painting by Bassano in exchange for his newly painted works. As the Bassano was the property of Sir Dudley's friend, Lord Henry Danvers, Rubens felt he could not afford to offend two august collectors, and agreed to the exchange. When the Bassano arrived, Rubens found to his chagrin that it was in a state of some deterioration; he responded to Sir Dudley offering instead a small wolf-hunting scene to be done by his own hand. This proved to be a much less satisfactory bargain than Sir Dudley had anticipated, so he requested something more. Rubens, himself quite adept in business matters, countered with a proposal to paint a larger canvas of lions instead of wolves, adding that, as noble lions would increase the picture's value, he would expect extra payment. Sir Dudley recognised defeat and promptly acquiesced.

The affair, however, did not end there. A report to Carleton from his agents Matthew and Trumbull who had arranged the transport of the completed pictures to England, informed him that 'The Lion Hunt' was not done entirely by Rubens' hand and, in fact, was the second version of a larger painting that had been sold to the Duke of Bavaria. Lord Danvers was incensed when he saw 'The Lion Hunt' as he had intended to present a splendid new painting by Rubens' own hand to the Prince of Wales, not a mere copy retouched by the master.

Rubens was most contrite when Sir Dudley wrote to him: 'We shall return your lions safely to you, and you shall send us tamer beasts better made.' Rubens offered to paint another picture in its place, but the animosity that had developed precluded mutual agreement. Eventually the Bassano was returned to Lord Danvers who in turn sent the Rubens back to Antwerp, thus concluding this unsatisfactory exchange.

The first monumental commission of Rubens' studio was begun in 1620, when he was forty-seven years of age. A contract was signed that called for thirty-six ceiling decorations and three retable paintings for the sumptuous new Jesuit church in Antwerp. The fee was to be 7,000 florins. Rubens put into this work a zeal that was surpassed only by that of Michelangelo in his painting of the Sistine Chapel. The physical discomfort that Michelangelo had endured was not shared in this instance, since Rubens relied heavily upon his assistants to carry out the work, and the paintings were done on canvas in the studio and later affixed to the ceilings of the church.

During a visit to Paris in 1622, Rubens signed a contract with Marie de Medici in which it was agreed that he would decorate two galleries in the new Luxembourg Palace for the sum of 20,000 crowns. The galleries were to be filled with a pageant of paintings in two series; one series was to illustrate important events in the life of Marie de Medici and the other was to depict events in the life of her murdered husband Henry IV. Sketches were made for the project and approved by Marie de Medici and the paintings were completed at his Antwerp studio within three years. The scope of the paintings demanded that Rubens exercise the full breadth of his inventive imagination; when they were completed fact had given way to richly decorative allegory.

Returning to Paris to supervise the installation of the Medici cycle of paintings, Rubens was introduced to the Duke of Buckingham, confidant to James I, and subsequently painted portraits of Buckingham and his wife. This rewarding relationship led to several commissions before the Duke's untimely assassination. Through Buckingham's instigation, Rubens completed nine paintings for the Banqueting House in Whitehall in 1634 on the theme of James I's reign. His son Charles I was guilty of tardiness in making payment for the series, as royal patrons sometimes were. Rubens displayed commendable patience in this matter—a wise attitude when dealing with kings.

Rubens' last great commission was a series of more than 100 paintings of subjects inspired by Ovid's *Metamorphoses* and *The Labours of Hercules*. His fertile imagination was stimulated by reading these books and the painting of these series gave him a glorious opportunity to depict nudes in every conceivable position. He painted these scenes with the assistance of Frans Snyders in 1636 for Philip IV's hunting lodge, the Toree de la Parada, near Madrid. In the same year he was appointed Court Painter to Philip's brother Ferdinand.

Rubens' last years were spent away from Antwerp as Lord of the Castle of Steen. The title was acquired with his purchase of this feudal estate situated in the country near Brussels. It was in this idyllic and rustic setting, away from the intrigues and stresses of court life, that Rubens was able to paint many pictures of his own choosing before his death in 1640.

Throughout history a few distinguished artists have developed a passionate interest in collecting works of art by other artists. By so doing, they actively encouraged and supported the careers of their fellows. Patronage may derive from the most eminent in the land, but one of the finest honours an artist may have conferred upon himself is recognition and appreciation by another member of his profession.

Rubens vies with Rembrandt in his achievements as an astute and passionate collector. In 1640 an inventory listed the works to be auctioned from Rubens' studio. Besides 300 of his own paintings, there were works from Van Dyck and his other principal assistants and associates. There were seventeen paintings by Adriaen Brouwer and several by Pieter Bruegel, Jan van Eyck and Lucas van Leyden, with numerous drawings and engravings. Rubens' will requested that his graphic works be withheld from sale in case a relative or descendant might become a painter and benefit from them.

CHAPTER 7

ACADEMIES OF ART

The aim of formal instruction in art is to prepare the student for a career as a professional artist; however, should he later decide to pursue another vocation, the experience of art study would have served to enrich his cultural background. Practice in the use of materials and techniques is fundamental to creation, while theoretical courses encourage exploration into the wider meaning and appreciation of art.

Workshop experience was formerly the accepted method of training for every artist, and had a great deal to commend it. An apprentice learned the practical aspects of the profession while contributing to workshop production. Workshops were worthwhile training-grounds if the master showed a strong interest in teaching, but the pressure of commissions frequently limited the time he could devote to it.

During the sixteenth century, centres for the teaching of art gradually shifted from individual workshops to established schools where policies were dictated by learned professionals who were associated with academies. For the first time public interest in the education and welfare of artists was aroused.

These first teaching institutions were established as an offshoot of the medieval guilds. The guilds had been formed for the purpose of protecting trade and the tradesman; the academies hoped to raise the status of the artist in society by teaching practical techniques and theories of art.

Conformity of thought within the guilds had led artists like Leonardo and Michelangelo to break from a system which they felt was restricting their freedom and individual genius. A new concept was sought which would elevate artists to a more prominent status than that of mere tradesmen. The opening of the first school of art instruction signalled the arrival of a new wind that was to ripple through the old studio workshop and change the tradition-bound craft of painting for ever.

As a result of the proliferation of art schools opening in all the major centres, the workshop master was no longer able to recruit apprentices who turned instead to the new institutions for a more formal training. In addition, economic factors diminished the number of commissions from important patrons. Staffs were reduced until finally the masters themselves were forced to take private pupils and to create pictures on a speculative basis without a specific commission.

Increasingly art was becoming channelled into new areas of study and research. The new centres of learning sought wider academic knowledge. Unlike the painters' associations of the past, they were not geared to the production of commissioned works of art. Students who attended academies for instruction were given set pieces on which to work in addition to attending lectures on art history, colour theory, perspective, anatomy and other relevant subjects. They endured criticism as a means of improving their techniques and benefited from the artistic knowledge of their teachers.

Well-endowed academies attempted to engage the leading exponents in each category of artistic endeavour as teachers. Those who succeeded in obtaining the services of painters of high reputation attracted a greater number of pupils. The artists who accepted teaching posts were generally those who felt that the experience would expand their horizons and challenge their minds. Many were engaged as part-time members of the faculty, teaching only one or two days a week, so that they were still able to continue their own creative work.

Several institutions formulated doctrines designed to separate the artist from the artisan. Instead of producing artists of talent, these schools became training-grounds for art teachers, historians and critics. Art had moved out of the realm of commercial fulfilment as a craft on to a more cultural plane. A legion of theoretical tacticians was now required who, although seldom painters themselves, were adequately equipped to write, criticise and lecture on all aspects of the subject.

THE EARLY ACADEMIES

The first important teaching institution about which there is substantial documentation was the school for students of painting and sculpture founded as an experiment by Lorenzo de Medici in his garden at Florence in about 1489. In contrast to the traditions of the guilds, the director and sculptor, Bertoldo, did not apprentice his pupils nor did their training include assisting him on commissioned work. He simply gave tuition based on a study of the antique and modern works in the Medici collection. It was into this setting that Michelangelo was introduced as a pupil by his first master, Ghirlandaio.

Leonardo da Vinci was the first great artist to be credited with the establishment of an art academy. Only fragmentary written evidence exists about the foundation of this institute, but six engravings bearing inscriptions relating to the *Accademia da Vinci* are still extant. Because of these prints, scholars surmise that a genius such as Leonardo was bound to have activated a teaching programme in order to project his many revolutionary ideas. Most likely, the principal subjects of this academy were architecture and the investigation of scientific phenomena. It is well known that Leonardo wished to elevate the arts from mere manual dexterity to a profound science.

It was not until 1563 that the first institution of academic instruction in the arts with a right to be properly called an academy was founded; this was the Accademia del Disegno in Florence, which is considered the prototype from which all subsequent art academies evolved. Its existence was due to the interest of Cosimo de Medici, the son of Giovanni, who suggested the institution's formation to the painter and biographer, Giorgio Vasari. A few years earlier the munificent Cosimo had given his official blessing to the Accademia Fiorentina, but this institute lacked an inspired administrator of the calibre of Vasari. Credit for Vasari's success at the new academy must be shared with the artists he originally recruited for his faculty. These included the painters Bronzino, Ghirlandaio, Granacci and Pontormo, the sculptors Ammananti and Rosi and other masters of such specialities as illumination, engraving and architecture. Through his fortuitous friendship with Michelangelo, Vasari assured the fame of his school by conferring upon this artist and Cosimo de Medici the honorary title of *Capi* of the institute.

In 1593 the Accademia di S. Luca was opened in Rome through the initiative of Cardinal Federico Borromeo and the painter Federico Zuccari. The original organisation of this academy compares favourably with the traditional teaching methods used in many art schools today. Tuition in drawing and painting from plaster casts and life was accompanied by theoretical discussion. Lectures for the students were opened to art connoisseurs from the public, thus broadening the institute's scope by establishing a positive community relationship. Like its predecessor the

Accademia del Disegno in Florence, the Accademia di S. Luca aspired to leadership in cultural affairs as well as taste and fashion.

As the influence of the first two important Italian academies gradually ebbed, a number of private schools calling themselves academies were inaugurated to supplant them. The members of these schools often met to draw nude models in painters' studios or in the houses of patrons, while maintaining a convivial relationship with the guilds. Perhaps the earliest and most notable of these was the Carracci studio-academy founded in Bologna in 1586. The three Carracci were Ludovico and his cousins Agostino and Annibale. Although they achieved fame as artists and teachers, their approach to teaching owed much to workshop environment and practice.

The success of the Italians in developing a structured art teaching programme led the Dutch painter and chronicler Carel Van Mander to establish an institution in Haarlem around 1600, modelled on these early academies.

In France the development of teaching methods evolved through a more systematic approach than in Italy. Although there was little difference in course content, the French attempted to arrange schedules that kept the students fully occupied and continually captivated. Regimentation of time and study was considered vital to ensure that the students developed good working habits. The structure of the faculty was closely co-ordinated to encourage a direct link with the students. This calculated effort to organise art training institutions along the lines of the great universities such as the Sorbonne, founded in the thirteenth century, paid off handsomely. The *académies* in France were a *tour de force* for more than 200 years.

The founding of the French Académie Royale de Peinture et de Sculpture in 1648 marked the beginning of one of the most influential institutions in the history of art. The Académie adhered to the fundamental practical and theoretical studies laid down by the insular Accademia di S. Luca; it encouraged students to travel and assimilate other cultures as well.

The establishment of awards such as the highly valued *Grand Prix* that granted promising students four years of study and residence at the Académie de France in Rome stressed the importance of intercultural experience. The Académie de France, founded in 1666 and an offshoot of the Académie Royale, owes its creation to motives that were less than entirely noble. One of the chief roles of the institution was the acquisition and shipment to France of as many works of antiquity as possible. Moreover, the painters and sculptors in residence were expected to copy the most famous paintings and statues for exhibition in the French museums.

The Académie Royale reached the apex of its glory and prestige under the flamboyant painter Charles LeBrun who became its director in 1683. Formal training at the Académie was famous for its emphasis on drawing; long and tedious periods of time were spent on making studies from plaster casts and uninspiring life poses. By 1689 a monthly examination of all the drawings that had been produced was imposed. From this arbitrary judging some pupils were rejected while others were promoted to more advanced levels. The Académie, functioning with royal assent, had established a virtual monopoly to the extent that private schools were forbidden and opposition was thrust aside. Yet this seemingly rigid programme was not totally inflexible; for a part of their training, pupils were sent to work and live in the studio of a master where they might learn painting, modelling and carving in an atmosphere reminiscent of that of the Middle Ages.

THE EIGHTEENTH CENTURY

During the eighteenth century there was a proliferation of academies founded in various art centres. Most of these were based upon the French pattern and followed a conventional programme of drawing, lectures on geometry, anatomy and perspective as well as copying the work of the masters. In addition, small private schools began to mushroom throughout Europe. They were generally something of a compromise between the workshop of old and the new academy. Pupils paid for tuition, although they often engaged in work for the master. The directors of these schools were usually artists who taught as a means of supplementing their income while awaiting commissions. Rembrandt's studio, for example, was used for the purpose of instruction and was typical of the type of private school that relied more on the reputation of its master than on its curriculum.

In 1711 Sir Godfrey Kneller was appointed the first governor of the Academy of Painting in London, which was conceived basically as a studio in which the pupils acted as assistants to a master and differed little from the conventional workshop.

The Royal Academy of Art was founded in 1768 by George III as a teaching institution and has remained so to this day. The original charter provided for forty academicians. In 1769 twenty associates were accepted and later this number increased to thirty.

From its inception, the Royal Academy was progressive in its thinking. Nude models of both sexes were permitted for life drawing studies. In contrast, the administrators of Madrid's Academia de S. Fernando, founded in 1753 by Philip V with Goya as its director, regarded this as too shocking and confined students to drawing from antique casts of the human body.

It is interesting to note that the founding of academies was not confined to Europe. Philadelphia was the site of a private school that was officially made the Pennsylvania Academy of Fine Arts in 1805. In Mexico the Real Academia de San Carlos de Neuva España had been opened as early as 1785.

ART AND REVOLUTION

The Académie continued to dictate the standards that artists were expected to attain. It maintained a sterile, tradition-bound teaching programme which tended to suppress any attempts at innovation by artists who had a capacity for individuality. The condemnation of painters who displeased this powerful alliance virtually prevented them from exhibiting their work in public. Even the Academicians themselves could incur the wrath of their fellows if they dared to exhibit elsewhere. Rejection by the Académie meant that the artist was without a shop-window for his work, as private art galleries were few and generally dealt in Old Master paintings or the work of approved Academicians. Official commissions, honours and teaching posts were granted only to those who were favoured by the Académie. This monopoly was finally broken following the French Revolution.

Fortunately, among the leaders of the Revolution had been men of vision who were determined to make works of art available to the public and to free the artists from the oppression of the Académie. Besides opening the doors of the Salon to wider participation, the Revolutionary Government decreed that a museum should be established in the Louvre and filled with treasures from palaces, monasteries and the great houses of France. Moreover, a generous sum of money was appropriated for the purchase of works of art.

Sadly, like many other phoenixes that have arisen out of the ashes of revolt, the Académie drifted back to its old dictatorial ways.

THE NINETEENTH CENTURY

At the beginning of the nineteenth century the Académie in France was still the arbitrary guardian of taste and style. Medals were awarded to those artists who found favour by following the prescribed edicts. In the latter half of the century the École des Beaux-Arts, which had been founded in 1648, was more closely allied with the Académie, thereby forming a coalition which presented a formidable barrier to artists outside the establishment. Intolerance in art was not confined to the venerable academicians of France; it was also the prevailing attitude of members of the Royal Academy in Britain and throughout most of Europe. The term 'academic' became, in the public view, synonymous with conservatism.

The academies unintentionally fostered a number of subsidiary schools, owing to the practice of many academicians of accepting promising students for further instruction at their own *ateliers*. Gradually, the more successful of these became independent art schools. The pupil's individuality often suffered from the indelible mark of masters who saw to it that their own styles and names were perpetuated by everyone who studied with them.

ART AND INDUSTRY

In the second half of the eighteenth century many art schools became allied with the various new industries that had emerged. By the late nineteenth century schools were encouraged and often financially supported by industry. Experts were recruited from the factories to teach the new, commercially viable art technology on a part-time basis. This was particularly true in Germany and Great Britain where industrialisation was gaining its greatest foothold.

An increasing need for a programme of art instruction tailored to the requirements of industry led to changes in the planning of new art schools. No longer was art solely a means of self-expression with the finished work an end in itself. Art was to be made a consumer product, an integral part of everyday life in the machine age. Even the exterior design and packaging of a product was subjected to market and cost analysis.

The Bauhaus, a school of architecture and applied art, was founded in Weimar in 1919 with Walter Gropius as its first director. It was one of the most important schools which based their courses on the unification of art and industry. The objective of this influential school was the evolution of production through the use of machines without the loss of quality that mechanisation implied. The faculty at the school in the 1920s included both Paul Klee and Wassily Kandinsky.

As the twentieth century dawned, the number of students who were vying to attain prominence in the art profession had reached saturation-point. The advent of the technological age offered art schools a reprieve from this dilemma. Schools began to include training programmes in industrial design, advertising art and other related subjects.

The academies had been superseded by schools of fine and commercial art that offered a practical approach to becoming a professional artist. In the past, the illusions of many young students who had hoped to make their careers as artists were dashed upon leaving school. Now those who possessed even a moderate talent found they could at least make a living in some field allied to their chosen profession.

CHAPTER 8

IMPRESSIONISM AND AFTER

The only reward one should offer an artist is to buy his work.
                                                    Pierre Auguste Renoir

Impressionism was an important artistic movement that flourished in France from the 1860s through the 1880s. Its goal was to achieve a completely naturalistic effect in painting by close observation of light and shadow and by the analysis of tone and colour. The painting techniques used by the Impressionists were a complete departure from those of the past. Paint was applied in small dabs and short flickering strokes in an *alla prima* manner; little or no underpainting was used and outlines of forms were left indistinct. The painter eliminated all non-essential detail to concentrate on the rhythms and colour harmony of his subject. The results were shimmering, high-key oil sketches with the bare canvas sometimes visible.

A precedent for the vigorous, uninhibited brushwork of the Impressionists had been set much earlier in art history when the Venetian painters experimented with fluid oil colours which they applied to their canvases in a free and highly spirited manner. The paintings of Tintoretto, and later Tiepolo, indicate the direction painting was to follow, although the planned composition persisted for nearly another three centuries.

In the seventeenth century the paintings of Frans Hals exhibited a freedom and flamboyancy of style that foreshadowed Impressionism. The popular 'Laughing Cavalier' demonstrates Hals' mastery of manipulating paint. The rich, luminous blacks of the cavalier's costume are painted with slashing strokes while the collar is created with interlaced white pigment. Viewed closely, there appears to be only a hint of detail; stepping back further, Hals' brushwork succeeds in creating an impression of intricate lacework, the execution of which might have occupied another painter for many hours. His brush darted here and there in an inspired manner—a true forerunner of Impressionism.

In 1874 several artists who shared similar ideas regarding a new direction in painting formed together to hold their first exhibition in the Paris studio of the photographer Nadar. They exhibited under the collective title of the 'Société Anonyme'. A journalist, reviewing the exhibition for *Les Charivari*, derisively called the group 'impressionists', after a painting by Monet called 'Impression Sunrise' (now in the Musée Marmottan, Paris). The name stuck and was accepted by the artists themselves.

The members of this elite band of revolutionaries included Paul Cézanne, Frédéric Bazille, Mary Cassatt, Edgar Degas, Armand Guillaumin, Édouard Manet, Claude Monet, Berthe Morisot, Camille Pissarro, Pierre August Renoir, Alfred Sisley and Georges Seurat. Strictly speaking a few of those mentioned are not classified by scholars as Impressionists; but they all exhibited and, at one time or another, collaborated in the movement's early phase. Vincent Van Gogh and Paul Gauguin share the convenient label of Post-Impressionists, implying their later arrival on the scene.

At that time it was the desire of all art students to have their paintings accepted by the Salon and eventually to become academicians. Numerous schools had been opened in Paris to cater for the aspiring artist. The Académie Suisse, opened by a model called Suisse, was the most renowned in Paris. It was actually an *atelier libre*, an open studio without a teacher where, for a small fee, students could work from a nude model. Cézanne, Guillaumin and Pissarro studied at the Académie Suisse; Bazille, Monet, Renoir and Sisley were enrolled at the Atelier Gleyre under the tutelage of the eminent painter Charles Gleyre.

The young students reproached for not painting in the approved manner soon found themselves without studios in which to work and receive instruction. Manet, rejected by Couture, set up his easel in the Louvre to paint from the Old Masters. Monet left the studio of Gleyre in 1863, taking Renoir, Sisley and Bazille with him to live and paint in the forest of Fontainebleau near Barbizon. The first famous French artists' colony was founded at Barbizon in the 1820s, where Millet was to spend the last twenty-five years of his life in retreat from political upheavals. Corot was another frequent resident of the colony. It was here that artists found the rustic simplicity that Rousseau had idealised.

Many tales are told concerning the beginnings of Impressionism. One of the most popular stories credits Monet with its discovery; supposedly Monet was painting one day and found he was without any black for rendering shadows. He used blue instead and Impressionism was born. The actual development of Impressionism came about with considerably more thought and study. Scientific investigations into the behaviour of light and the development of chemically manufactured pigments paved the way for painting out-of-doors. The Impressionists studied the varying effects of light in all its aspects, and the new types of paints gave them colours with an extended range of spectral nuances that had not been available before. Above all, the collapsible metal tube, which had become universally obtainable, initiated a major innovation in oil painting. Artists were liberated from the tedious task of grinding and preparing pigments as they could be purchased ready made from colour merchants. The small bladder that for centuries had been used to store pigments became obsolete. Landscape artists at last had a most satisfactory means of transporting fresh paint. The irreplaceable studio easel was given an auxiliary companion—a portable easel with adjustable legs that enabled the artist to set up on any precipitous terrain.

OPEN-AIR PAINTING

Among the first major artists to work out-of-doors was the nineteenth-century English painter John Constable. Constable painted delightfully free compositions of the English countryside. These spontaneous paintings were small and sketchily executed. Later, in the studio, he sometimes used them as preliminary studies for large, more carefully executed paintings with which he hoped to catch the eye of the judges of the Royal Academy Exhibition.

During this era the studio became a base camp from which the Impressionists sallied forth on punitive expeditions to confront nature and capture her many moods. Capes, berets and muddied boots were as much part of the paraphernalia of the open-air painter's studio as were the folding easel, camp stool and umbrella.

No effort was too great for the truly impassioned painter who revelled in his new-found freedom. Renoir required the services of several friends each day to help carry his large canvas and equipment from the studio to the dance hall where he painted his famous composition 'Le Bal au Moulin de la Galette'. Renoir frequented the Moulin de la Galette and it was here he met many of the young girls who eventually modelled for him. For his

Page 107 (left) 'A Painter's Studio' by A. van Ostade, a typical seventeenth century studio in the Netherlands. *(right)* 'Cupid Complaining to Venus' by Lucas Cranach; a painting by the art factory master of a slim-hipped Venus with sensuous, elongated limbs in the style that brought him fame

Page 108 'Hélène Four|
ment in a Fur Coat' b|
Rubens, *c* 1631. Ruber|
captures the radiant ser|
suality of his youn|
second wife; her skir|
pearly white and ros|
tinged, catches the ligh|
in a way that was to ir|
fluence Renoir mor|
than two centuries late|

painting 'Women in the Garden', Monet dug a trench in his garden at Ville d'Avray into which he could lower an enormous canvas with a pulley. The canvas was eased into the trench whenever he wished to paint the top area of the picture. While executing his two famous series of haystacks and cathedrals, Monet painted at the same hour on successive days in order to capture the effects of the fleeting light. He spent several weeks waiting for just the correct weather conditions appropriate to each picture.

The problems of painting in the open were diverse and numerous. A painter standing in a field might find passers-by gathering round to chat and watch him at work. Cézanne is reported to have bolted with canvas, easel and umbrella in disarray at the sight of an onlooker approaching him. Not the least of the difficulties were gusts of wind that made the canvas act like a ship's sail, often tipping the easel over. Artists with a penchant for winter landscapes had to be prepared for a personal chilling and for harden- ing of the oil colours. Working under a hot summer's sun creates another difficulty; the concentration required to capture a particular light effect before it changes invites a physical tension and body fatigue which is vir- tually unknown in the studio. The intensity of the sun may become so great that distant fields blur before the eyes in a shimmering heat haze. One can appreciate the sun-obsessed Van Gogh's anxiety to finish pictures quickly.

After long sessions of exposure to the elements the painter would return to his studio to examine his outdoor endeavours away from the glare of the sun and remove from the still wet paint flies, gnats and dust.

STUDIOS AND FRIENDS

The Impressionists' studios also served as meeting-places where members of the group gathered to discuss theoretical problems of painting. In their self-portraits artists often depicted themselves in the studio as a convivial group surrounding one of their number while he painted. They used fellow artists and friends as models and often painted each other working in the open.

Patronage for the Impressionists was virtually non-existent; but few patrons can have endeared themselves to artists more than did the ordinary men of small means who believed in them despite the denunciations of the critics. One of the small band of supporters of the Impressionists was the colour merchant Père Tanguy. The name and likeness of the kindly Père Tanguy are perpetuated in Van Gogh's portrait of the little colour mer- chant sitting with hands clasped in front of a wall literally papered with a

7

display of Japanese prints. Before opening his shop in Paris, Père Tanguy had been an itinerant paint salesman who took his merchandise to the forest of Fontainebleau where he met Monet, Renoir and Pissarro on several occasions. Tanguy accepted the unsaleable work of Van Gogh, whom he befriended—just as he had accepted Cézanne's paintings in lieu of payment for canvases and pigments.

Another true patron was Victor Choquet, a civil servant in the customs administration, who was of modest means but elegant taste. For small sums Choquet purchased many canvases from Renoir, Monet and, in particular, Cézanne, from whom he acquired thirty-one paintings. Both Choquet and Tanguy were visionaries who saw beyond the fashionable art of their epoch and offered encouragement and friendship to the artists at a time when others ridiculed their work.

The Impressionists were constantly seeking landscape locations in which to paint. This search sometimes took them far afield and they were obliged to find studios nearby with favourable light and amenities. After renting a studio in the Rue de Vaugirard in Paris, Frédéric Bazille wrote of the owner giving him access to a small garden: 'it is most pleasant in summer for painting people in the sunlight!' Painting in gardens gave the artists time to study light effects in the open away from the gaze of onlookers while the proximity of their studios proved a considerable convenience.

Visible remains of one of the greatest movements of art history are to be found in the still-preserved homes of Cézanne, Renoir and Monet. These dwellings form a link with the past and reveal some indication of the characters of the three artists and their life-styles.

CÉZANNE'S STUDIO

Cézanne's house near Aix-en-Provence, now a Cézanne museum, contains one of the few studios still intact, just as the dour and taciturn artist left it. Unlike the studios of Rembrandt, Rubens and other great masters of the more distant past, Cézanne's workplace has not been rearranged. There remains an air of authenticity, as if the owner were about to enter, collect his folding easel, beret and rucksack (still hanging in the corner), and depart on another painting foray.

Cézanne's vast, high-ceilinged studio, occupying the entire second floor of the house, is large enough to have allowed him to work on his enormous canvas 'Les Grandes Baigneuses' which occupied him for more than seven years. Many of the objects he used in his still-life paintings—bottles and jars of various shapes, a wooden mannikin, skulls on shelves, a rosary, paints, palettes and bottles of turpentine—are preserved in this room. His home was totally without luxury; all of the objects in it were utilitarian, as Cézanne was singularly devoted to painting.

In all probability, the irascible Cézanne turned to still life when he became exasperated with models who tired of posing. His famous portrait of the publisher Ambroise Vollard was completed only after over one hundred sittings and still it appears sketchily executed. Cézanne was fortunate to have been provided with a small income for life by his father; therefore he did not have to rely on commissions or the sale of his work to sustain his modest style of living.

So much has been written about Cézanne's painting that it is perhaps best left to Cézanne himself to evaluate his motives and aspirations: 'Our art, should convey the thrill of nature's continuity, with the appearance of its changes. It should enable us to feel nature as eternal . . . I want to paint nature as though no one had ever painted it before.' How admirably prophetic are these words from the man who laid the foundations for art in the twentieth century.

RENOIR'S STUDIO

Amidst the gentle sunlit hills of Cagnes high above the Mediterranean stands 'Les Collettes' which for nearly twenty years was the home of Pierre Renoir. The house and garden have been opened to the public as a museum.

The grounds of the estate are shaded with pines and gnarled olive trees. In this rustic setting, Renoir passed his final years painting landscapes. His son Jean Renoir tells us: 'Renoir would have himself carried to the studio, or be taken around to look for a "Landscape" or else finish one he had already begun'. Sometimes he painted in a specially constructed glassed shed, no more than five yards wide, which was situated among the olive trees.

In front of the house stands 'Venus', one of Renoir's loveliest sculptures, seemingly presiding over the residence as a symbol of his devotion to the beauty of the female form. Inside, the rooms still seem to echo the voices of the happy family atmosphere and tranquillity that once prevailed. Visitors climb the stairs to Renoir's windowed studio with much the same feeling of awe and reverence that they might experience when approaching a religious shrine.

It is here in the studio that the presence of Renoir is most strongly felt. Everything has been preserved just as he left it, for he painted actively until his death; the easel, a couch for posing models, paints, and brushes are kept in the customary orderliness he maintained throughout his life. Most poignant of all is the wheelchair to which he was confined in his final years, standing empty in the room. It is a reminder of the indomitable spirit which spurred his frail body to paint continuously although crippled with painful arthritis.

A sign beside the villa gate provides a fitting epitaph for the painter whose work has brought such great pleasure to people everywhere:

> Here for 20 years lived Pierre Auguste Renoir, artist and painter, born at Limoges in 1841, died at Cagnes in 1919. His works, distributed throughout the entire world, have brought glory to Cagnes.

MONET'S STUDIO

Monet's studio is in Giverny only a few miles from Paris. It was in Giverny that he spent the second half of his life, until 1926 when he died at the age of eighty-six. The house and separate studio building are still preserved, but it was the vast garden that was Monet's real studio. The grounds contain an abundant and stunning variety of flowers, shrubs and trees, providing a profusion of colour to greet the eye. Dozens of Japanese woodcut prints paper the walls of the entrance to his studio where once stood the paintings of 'Nympheas,' or 'Waterlilies' from his pond, vibrant in the half-light. Monet's quest for the sensations of light and purity of tone is fully expressed in this remarkable series of paintings which, in their fleeting effects and fragmented colour, anticipate the modern Abstract Expressionist movement. The Japanese influence dominates the interior decor of the house; the yellow-painted dining-room is decorated with banks of Japanese prints. It is difficult to reconcile the Monet of pastoral calm and serenity at Giverny with the Monet who had written earlier: 'I have just been turned out of my room, naked as a worm. I do not know where I shall sleep tomorrow.'

CHAPTER 9

THE MODERN STUDIO

The advent of the Impressionist movement had established the new role of the studio as a meeting-place. The artist became a complete individualist. With few clients to purchase his works he did not require a workshop or assistants and his only need of collaboration might be to meet with fellow artists to discuss the progress of their new movement.

The art market has always demanded a multitude of images from the artists in fashion. Today, some well-known contemporary artists have found it necessary to employ assistants in the studio in order to meet the demand for their work. This return to the centuries-old tradition of the workshop brings the history of the studio full circle.

Collaboration in the arts has often proven successful throughout the long course of art history. Perhaps the most unusual story of an artist's dependence upon the skills of another is that of Renoir and his only assistant. During his latter years Renoir was stricken with an arthritic infirmity; his hands were incapable of the arduous tasks of sculpting and modelling. Eventually Renoir was introduced to a talented young Italian sculptor whom he employed to assist him. Visitors to the studio were greeted by the sound of murmurs and grunts as Renoir, seated in his wheelchair, indicated to his helper the depth of penetration of each desired gouge. Renoir's sculptural works, although few in number, are a remarkable translation of his drawings and paintings of female figures in the round. This close collaboration and fusion of two artistically inspired beings has barely been surpassed.

Artists in our technological age may seek the services of craftsmen who are skilled in working with recently developed materials. This is particularly true of sculptors who now have a wealth of synthetic substances from which to choose for their creations. Hammer, chisel and stone have made way for polyester resins, plastics and welded metals. Lacking the necessary technical knowledge and skill in manipulating these materials, the contemporary sculptor may hire specialist craftsmen to follow his designs, much as an architect does when commissioning a firm of builders to carry out his plans.

Today painters are faced with similar problems. Just as the traditional tools and materials of the sculptor are sometimes superseded, so too are the painters' brushes, oils and painting supports. Painters are now using virtually every surface and substance possible for creating new imagery. A danger lies in most artists being unaware of the response of new materials to stress, atmospheric conditions and ageing. Many materials which have been adapted by artists were originally designed for quite different purposes, and their longevity in art terms has yet to be proved.

STUDIO INTERIORS

Few painters are fortunate enough to have studios designed expressly for the purposes of creative art. Ideally, the modern studio should be located at the top of a building in order to capture available light. A large, angled skylight with blinds for increasing or reducing natural light is desirable. The French design of a single-room studio with living accommodation on a balcony is still one of the most compact and convenient arrangements for an artist with modest means.

More often a studio is improvised from a room in the home, but one essential requirement remains—there must be sufficient light. The famous north light was prized by artists in the nineteenth century as they were particularly concerned with having light in the studio that was comparable with natural daylight. North light is less variable as the sun rises in the east and sets in the west; therefore, it is more consistent as the sun does not shine directly into the studio.

In the past the lack of suitable illumination at night made painting strictly a daylight occupation. However, the creative urge of certain intrepid artists, such as Michelangelo and Van Gogh, drove them to work at night by candlelight. Nowadays, artists may use fluorescent lighting and special lamps which simulate daylight.

Practical furnishings and objects in a contemporary studio may include, apart from easels and paints, a mirror for viewing paintings in reverse and a folding step ladder for large-scale works. Most studios contain a variety of still-life subject-matter such as vases and bottles. The Italian painter,

Giorgio Morandi filled his workplace with a lifetime's collection of bottles of every size, shape and colour, many of which may be identified in his paintings.

The availability of art books, reproductions and related printed matter has increased immensely in the last century. Few contemporary studios are without a collection. The titles often give an indication of the artist's particular interests, whether they be reference books on materials, techniques, anatomy or art aesthetics and criticism. Through reproductions and publications, the artist can have at his fingertips the accumulated knowledge of generations from Cennino Cennini's fifteenth-century treatise to the latest experiments with synthetic paints,

In the past, painters have devised various forms of mental detachment while engaged in painting. Rubens frequently had someone read to him from the classics while he worked, and by this means he continued to absorb and learn while painting. Some Italian masters were fond of musical accompaniment in their studios. The painter today is more likely to be soothed by a radio or hi-fi tape-recorder playing music to suit his mood. A few painters even attempt to watch television while they work.

It is quite usual for artists to employ the camera. Pop art, which is derived from advertising art, exploits photo-imagery and reproduction techniques to their fullest extent. The types of camera employed by artists range from large plate-holding cameras on tripods to cinematic or hand-held roll film cameras. Perhaps the most useful aid has been the Polaroid instant print which has proved of immense value to artists.

A conspiracy of silence has kept secret the use of photography by several famous painters. Cézanne, the father of modern painting, worked from photographs on occasion. This information was suppressed by dealers and critics who feared it might reflect unfavourably upon his reputation. The art critic Robert Hughes, writing about the French artist Edouard Vuillard, says:

> Vuillard was, in fact, one of the first artists to use a Kodak systematically. It was his habit to set up his camera and focus it while talking to friends, and startle them with a cry of 'One moment, please!' and a click. Much of the angling and perspective in Vuillard's rooms seems to correspond to the distortions of an old-fashioned lens.

When the colour reproduction process came into use for books and art reproductions, gloom prevailed in the art world. It seemed that the artist's original work would be superseded, but this forecast has not proved true.

Art reproductions have, in fact, stimulated the sale of original paintings. Many collectors bought reproductions in the early stages of their art appreciation; as their interest and knowledge of art developed, these reproductions were eventually replaced by original works.

Perhaps one of the most famous artists who used photographic images as inspiration for his oil paintings was the recluse, Maurice Utrillo. A large collection of picture-postcard views of Paris provided the main source of his subject matter. He worked in a tiny studio producing numerous evocative paintings of Parisian streets and buildings in which the paint was trowelled on with palette knives in an imitation of cement and plaster.

THE PICASSO LEGEND

A working day during the life of Pablo Picasso might have been visualised as a Hollywood film dream sequence: the master enters his graphic studio; on his left, a row of lithographic stones is laid side by side on a table; on his right, a row of similarly placed copper plates are prepared for etching. Two intent technicians stand ready to transpose his every drawn line into etched reality as Picasso moves forward to make his drawings upon stone and copper. The completed works are then taken to graphic studios in Paris where master printers will pull large editions from each stone or plate. Once approved by the master, the final prints are, upon occasion, signed by a secretary who expertly imitates Picasso's signature to spare the master's time and strength for his next creative venture.

Moving on to an adjacent studio, the master greets a group of ceramic craftsmen who stand by to offer their advice and assistance. Picasso plunges his hands into the prepared clay and in a burst of controlled energy he completes several sculptures and pots, evoking the style of early Mediterranean cultures. The morning's production is carried to a factory kiln for glazing, firing and making moulds from which to cast reproductions.

At last Picasso enters the painting studio where he can work unassisted. As he stands concentrating before a canvas, a furrowing of the brow indicates the nucleus of an idea about to stir the great hand. And so would begin another epic film in the creation of art, genius and myth, accompanied on sound track by mysterious music of the East and narration from a voice sounding as if it came from within the Oracle.

A fantasy? No, not entirely. Despite his passing, the prodigious talents of Picasso remain the hub of a great world-wide business still thriving on the legacy of his enormous output. Almost every working day of his life

Picasso had helped produce millions of francs worth of art objects for the world market. His merest daub or the rag he wiped his brush on, had a value; even his waste baskets and dustbins outside the villa gate were often searched in the hope of finding an 'original'.

This private, yet very public, artist was without any real idea of, or interest in, his personal accumulation of wealth. The major profits were made by his dealers, associates and others on the fringe of his talent. He was a victim of his own fame. Given equipment and a place to work, his needs were fulfilled; only time was of the essence and some of this had to be sacrificed to the demands of publicity to perpetuate the legend.

In order to gain more time for creative work, Picasso's enormous output was produced with the help of assistants. For example, the Paris firm of Fernand Mourlot has printed Picasso's lithographs since 1947 when he first used the process extensively. Henri Deschamps, the chief craftsman at Mourlot's, was entrusted by Picasso not only to supervise the printing of his lithographs, but also to translate his drawings directly on to zinc plates.

The use of assistants is not in itself a deception. The fact that the hand of the master has not produced the final version of a work is not unjustifiable. The artist is the originator, supplying the inspiration for the work; he is often the supervisor of its progress and, upon completion, his satisfaction is the final approval. The work is representative of him and will bear his signature or cypher, or will simply be acknowledged as his by its individual style.

Dealers and agents sell, besides original work, Picasso art reproductions, sculpture, pottery, publications and films. In addition, place-mats, tea towels, ashtrays, scarves—in fact, almost any commercial product—may bear Picasso's motifs for a price. This vast enterprise involves many people whose orbits have revolved round the master's production. It has been claimed that Picasso's dealer Kahnweiler hoarded away in a warehouse a huge number of canvases as yet unseen by the public. These have been culled from different stylistic periods. Now that Picasso is dead these works are to be offered periodically to the market at even more grossly inflated prices than his work fetched during his lifetime. A large organisation of print-sellers has similar plans; they invested more than a million pounds in his original etchings and lithographs which they intend to make available.

Alexander Lieberman, in his book *The Artist in His Studio*, described an actual visit he made to Picasso's vast studio in Vallauris, once a perfume factory but now abandoned:

Picasso, perhaps fearing that he will lose a source of inspiration, never allows anything to be thrown away. His houses, his studios show the accumulation of his long life. Picasso needs all the memorabilia, all the art and sculpture of the world to inspire him, but to produce he needs little. All has to be reduced to essentials as uncluttered as the inspirational sources were cluttered. His tools are a few brushes, a few squeezed tubes, some paint pots, a bottle or two of turpentine and oil, small tablets for palettes: 'I use very little oil—mostly turpentine. I make all my own small palettes out of plywood. I use boat paint—any kind they give me.' This is all Picasso needs in order to create. The rest is in his mind.

Many restorers might throw up their hands in despair at Picasso's admission of the inconsequence with which he regarded his painting materials. Yet, it is true; many well-known artists have shown disregard for the permanency of their materials. Because of this attitude the works of many modern artists are prone to deterioration at a more rapid rate than those of the methodical and technically correct Old Masters.

Picasso's several outbuildings that functioned as studios have their counterpart in a single room in the home of Georges Braque, according to Lieberman:

> Braque divides his studio into separate areas, like the stage of the mystery dramas in the Middle Ages: areas for engraving, for drawing and water colour, for relaxation and, the largest, for painting. On several easels, I saw different canvases simultaneously in progress. They looked like parts of the studio, the studio like parts of the paintings. There was no divorce.

Picasso and several other modern masters owe a small debt of gratitude to the skills of the French etcher Jacques Villon, who later achieved a considerable reputation as a modern printmaker and painter. In the 1920s, Villon was commissioned by the Bernheim Jeune Gallery in Paris to undertake the formidable task of preparing more than forty coloured intaglio etchings after paintings by Picasso, Matisse, Cézanne, Manet and others. Several years of work were involved in the preparation of the plates, but the results were so superb that Villon was recognised as the outstanding living technician in graphic art—a fact that kept his own career as an artist moribund. One wonders if the potential for individual artistic expression of many assistants might be stifled by their remaining in the shadows cast by better-known masters.

ART FACTORIES

The demand for inexpensive paintings as decorations for homes and business premises has increased steadily since the eighteenth century; however, the production-line approach to supplying uninspired works of art for an undiscriminating public has existed for much longer. Dutch artists were among the first to paint pictures with the average citizen in mind. It was not until more than a century later that truly banal paintings were turned out *en masse* without any pretence of inherent quality or artistic concept; quick sales and a rapid turnover were the only concerns. Accomplished artists who found themselves in financial difficulty were sometimes compelled to engage in this rather repugnant trade. Gustave Courbet, for example, spent his last years eking out an existence in charge of a studio producing 'picture-postcard' paintings of Swiss landscapes.

In Germany and Austria there are a number of art factories which regularly churn out uninspired works for the masses. The pictures generally depict scenes of the Romantic school—mountains by moonlight and lakes reflecting clouds and trees. These gaudily-coloured pictures find an audience, particularly in the tourist centres. The paintings are mass-produced on an assembly-line basis with each artist successively contributing his own speciality to each picture. One artist may render a lake while another paints mountains, a third strokes in the sky and then passes the picture to the last artist, who, in a rapid staccato of brushwork, adds bushes and trees.

In other studios, one artist may paint the entire picture; he may specialise in a dozen or more scenes which he repeats over and over again in identical colours and style. The need to earn a living sometimes attracts quite talented artists to this soul-destroying occupation. The artist's initial enthusiasm departs after several hundred copies have been made. A scene which at first was well painted may soon become a thin veneer of its earlier inspiration.

Many factory paintings are often no more than hand-painted photographic enlargements. Scenes and portraits taken with a camera can be transferred to specially sensitised canvas-textured surfaces. Workshop artists then paint with oils over the monochrome composition, using colour photographic prints of the subject as a guide. This practice comes perilously close to the painting-by-numbers kits found in toy shops.

Not all art factories are located in large cities. Several European rural areas, relatively isolated until recent years, have become centres of 'peasant art' or 'naïve painting'. Peasant families, whose daily lives are taken up with farming, spend their spare time painting for distant, sophisticated markets.

Generations of farmer-painters in Czechoslovakia, Rumania and Yugo-slavia have produced pictures, at first for pleasure, then for profit. In the last few years many of them have forsaken the fields in order to paint full-time. Dealers comb the countryside in search of new talent which they may exploit, frequently purchasing the works of an entire village wholesale. Unfortunately much of the naïve charm of these pictures has diminished as a result of the peasant painters' eagerness to comply with the art market's demands.

The acquisition of large quantities of original, cheaply-purchased paint-ings by untutored amateurs is not confined to dealers travelling in remote regions; Scandinavian dealers regularly visit art academies in Paris to buy paintings by young students. The canvases are bought by the hundreds—nudes and still-life studies, landscapes and abstracts. The paintings are removed from their stretchers and stacked in piles for shipment to Sweden, Norway and Denmark where they are exhibited in galleries as genuine 'école de Paris'.

Paris, so long the *grande dame* of the art world, has played hostess to many great artists; she has also harboured hoards of art mercenaries. Many painters seen copying from the Old Masters in the Louvre and other museums do so, not out of love for the old techniques, but simply because they have been commissioned by a part of the antique trade which deals in 'original' copies. A few artists paint in the museums in hopes of meeting potential clients who may commission them to copy additional pictures from the collection. To safe-guard the possibility that one of these copies might one day be mistaken for the original painting, the museums insist that the size of the copy must be slightly smaller or larger than the original.

The tourist attraction of Montmartre abounds with artists who, often in the traditional garb of beret and smock, appear to be painting views of the famed church of Sacre Coeur. In reality, some of these artists may be shills posing to attract spectators whom they hope to persuade into near-by gal-leries. The gallery invariably sells factory-system paintings and the 'artist' receives a percentage of any resulting sales. Superficiality in the arts, as in other aspects of life, is unfortunately becoming the *malaise* of the twentieth century.

The art factories of Europe are not without their parallel in the United States where an additional interesting variation of this industry exists—the one-man factory artist who travels from place to place in the manner of the American itinerant portrait painter. On arrival in a town, the artist usually sets up his easel and previously painted pictures in an empty shop for which the landlord is paid a modest fee or given a painting. The artist paints repetitious scenes in a variety of sizes while standing in the shop-front window in full view of passers-by. A sign indicates that there are more inexpensive framed originals within. The painter's ability to paint a scene deftly in oils in less than ten minutes is a sure-fire attraction and sales soon result. Without this display of American enterprise and showmanship, it is unlikely that many of these pot-boilers would sell.

A commercial successor of the Old Masters' workshop might well be the modern cartoon studio made famous by Hollywood. This vast industry has been extended to many lands and employs thousands of people in dream factories working to produce a modern folk art. The growth of television has expanded the use of commercial art and animation which in turn has provided employment for a legion of artists and technicians.

SCULPTURE STUDIOS

Many modern sculptors find that additional space is required to accommodate their large-scale work. Some sculptors have had to convert factory premises, warehouses or even aircraft hangars. Assistants are nearly always needed for carrying out these grandiose projects. Henry Moore and other sculptors of international repute are literally besieged by students who wish to assist them.

A new breed of sculptor has arrived in recent years in the form of young students who are already exhibiting and gaining recognition. Their experience is limited to providing working drawings for skilled technicians who construct the sculpture using materials the student cannot manipulate himself.

Foundries have also developed in new directions. There is at present a firm from which one can order original sculpture directly by telephone; a do-it-yourself kit is provided by post that contains a number of small-scale shapes which may be joined in unlimited permutations. A telephone call is then made to the firm quoting the numbers of the parts and their locations on a multi-lined grid supplied with the kit. These are assembled at the factory on a larger scale using modular sections in a variety of materials ranging from wood to metal or plastic and in a selection of colours.

Traditional foundries that cast in bronze sometimes set aside an area of their premises for selected artists to work on their models. The sculptor may act as assistant to the foundry worker during the process of casting and finishing his piece. Another aspect of work undertaken by some foundries is the translation of wood and stone sculptures into bronze casts. Sometimes these 'original replicas' are authorised by the artist's dealer, his family, or a foundry director, to be cast long after the artist has died.

MULTIPLES

The dictionary defines the word 'multiple' as containing or consisting of more than one; repeated more than once; manifold. Few in the art world would quarrel with this definition, although it might now include today's multiple art movement. An artist who speaks of multiples is usually referring to objects which are mass-produced (often in unlimited editions), unnumbered, probably unsigned, and sold inexpensively.

Multiples in art are hardly new. What is new is the current concept of that age-old question, 'what is art?' Today, art may be a worn toothbrush or a lavatory seat, mass-produced as an art form from synthetic materials for the supposed artistic edification of a large populace. Apparently no object is too mundane to be reproduced. In the past, multiples were created for a very real market. Sometimes the works were of significance, sometimes they were not, but their common feature was sincerity of purpose.

Multiples in painting now seem almost traditional in comparison with the glut of machine-stamped and packaged articles produced by the purveyors of urban art for the masses. The undisputed king of multiple paintings was the American art entrepreneur Martin Lowitz who, in the 1960s, sold in excess of 100,000 original paintings a year. He had a stable of independent artists working for him in various parts of the world whose main qualification was the ability to paint exceptionally fast in a variety of styles—some reminiscent of Picasso, Braque, Matisse, or one of the other famous modern masters. Other painters worked for special effects, such as palette-knife painting with heavy impasto or Impressionistic daubs. A limited number of stock sizes were used for the paintings to simplify framing and speed up distribution. The clients were usually large hotel chains who ordered pictures by the hundreds to fill every room of their establishments in different parts of the country. Newly proposed banks, cinemas, department stores and restaurants became potential clients as soon as an architect was engaged. One hazard was that the paintings were frequently stolen, but that meant additional business for Mr Lowitz and his painting stable who were always ready with replacements.

Some of the artists in the multiple painting business work under contract, using pseudonyms in order to remain anonymous for fear that their reputations as fine artists may be sullied by their association with such a commercial enterprise. The need for secretiveness is less vital today when the marriage of commercial art and fine art seems to have become finalised by the acceptance of the pop art movement.

Andy Warhol, the wonder-boy of pop art, came to the public's attention in the 1960s with his paintings of soup tins and multiple silk-screen images of Marilyn Monroe. Warhol, incidentally, carries out all of his various art and filming activities in a building appropriately called 'The Factory'. Warhol's artistic philosophy is summed up by his belief that an artist should not be too close to his work, which is why he employs others to do it for him.

Victor Vasarely, an artist of international repute, maintains a large workshop with assistants to channel his optical design ideas into visual form. Bridget Riley is another artist who deals with complex optical imagery. Much of her work is sketched on graph paper which is then translated and enlarged on to other surfaces by studio technicians. A single unit is repeated to form a multiple design in mathematically inspired optical illusions of space and movement.

The prices of signed multiples by famous contemporary artists have not yet descended to the level of many original paintings. Until they do, perhaps reproductions of these multiples will have to be made for the less prosperous collectors! Chaotic confusion in trying to distinguish a reproduction from a multiple from an original should be ensured amongst art scholars for years to come.

ORIGINAL PRINTS

It is in the area of artists' original prints, etchings, lithographs, woodcuts and serigraphy (silk screen) that some justifiable confusion arises over what is multiple and what is original. It is here that the knowledge and integrity of the artist, dealer and other experts must rule supreme in the quest for clarity. Each print approved by the artist and taken from a plate or other graphic surface may be considered an original. Only a monoprint (a single impression) is unique.

The definition of an original print according to the recommendations of the Print Council of America is as follows:

1   The artist alone has made the image in or upon the plate, stone, wood block or other material, for the purpose of creating a work of graphic art.

2 The impression is made directly from that original material, by the artist or pursuant to his directions.

3 The finished print is approved by the artist.

This set of standards serves merely as a guide and does not dictate any limitations upon the number of original prints that may be made from an edition. Therefore it implies that this may be left to the artist's discretion, since the individual graphic process he employs may, in itself, limit the number of impressions which may be pulled from a continually wearing surface.

The limiting of editions by signing and numbering each print has been practised only during the past century. None of the great master print-makers such as Dürer, Rembrandt or Goya used this system; consequently, some prints of inferior quality that were printed in later centuries from worn plates have come on the market.

A signed work by an artist will nearly always sell for a greater amount than an unsigned one. In some instances this has led to practices which have unnecessarily confused the graphic scene still further. Reproductions of artists' graphics and original paintings (watercolours in particular) can achieve a remarkable similarity to the original, particularly when printed on paper of identical texture, size and weight. Some of these reproductions have been issued in limited editions with each print signed individually by well-known artists. Although most of the prints bear the firm's stamp and are identifiable by this as reproductions, a great many people incorrectly believe that they are purchasing an original work. Auction house experts are regularly confronted by collectors who have carefully kept these pictures for years. They find it hard to believe that their treasures are only reproductions.

Artists' original prints have long suffered by being classed together as 'lithographs', a title of convenience used by staffs in many galleries. This is often a sign that they either lack knowledge of graphic processes or fear that the word 'print' may have the connotation of reproduction in the mind of a client. Lithography is an individual process, as are etching, wood engraving, serigraphy or other graphic methods. An original graphic print has every chance of increasing in value, but people mainly buy graphic images because they like them and for no other reason.

Page 125 (above) The great studio in Rubens' house in Antwerp; today it is a museum, but it once echoed to the voices of the Master and his assistants working in feverish activity. *(below)* 'Monet Painting in His Garden at Argenteuil' by Pierre August Renoir, 1873

Page 126 (left) 'The Studio: A Real Allegory of the Last Seven Years of My Life as an Artist' by Gustave Courbet; a detail from this huge canvas shows Courbet at his easel with a nude model and a small boy who acts as the innocent onlooker. The painting in its entirety is filled with figures from various walks

CHAPTER 10

THE ARTIST TODAY

Painting is complete as a distraction. I know of nothing which, without
exhausting the body, more entirely absorbs the mind . . .

Winston S. Churchill

MOTIVATION

The desire to create lasting works of art has guided man's mind and hand
since time immemorial. The fact that a work of art may be non-utilitarian
in man's daily life is inconsequential; he has created an object which is
pleasing to himself and appreciated by his fellows, and which will, he hopes,
be pleasing to succeeding generations.

In the past the status of an artist was generally one which commanded
respect, but, even during times when it was not, the artist could at least
expect to have steady employment and remuneration. A fine-art career
nowadays is regarded as a precarious pursuit, fraught with financial anxiety.
Yet the creative impulse burns intensely; heedless of privation, an increasing number of aspirants pursue their destinies to become artists.

The contemporary artist seems compelled to invent a new language in
art based upon his own interests and aspirations, which he hopes will
excite and enlighten society. New public symbols have replaced the traditional ones of yesteryear which were familiar to everyone. Whereas painting was once directed towards the service of the community, church or
state, it is now generally a means of self-expression, fulfilling the artist's
own desires.

If quality were determined by sheer enthusiasm on the part of the
painter, then certainly many amateurs would have the right to be called
professional artists. Amateur painters constitute a larger group than professionals in many communities. The pleasure to be derived from an art

hobby is best expressed by one of the greatest exponents of amateur painting, Winston Churchill, who wrote about his experiences in his book
Thoughts and Adventures. The chapter entitled 'Painting as a Pastime' was
subsequently published as a booklet incorporating reproductions of the
great man's paintings. Churchill defined the difference between the amateur
and the professional quite vividly:

> Two years of drawing-lessons, three years of copying woodcuts, five
> years of plaster casts—these are for the young. They have enough to bear.
> And this thorough grounding is for those who, hearing the call in the
> morning of their days, are able to make painting their paramount lifelong
> vocation. The truth and beauty of line and form which by the slightest
> touch or twist of the brush a real artist imparts to every feature of his
> design must be founded on long, hard, persevering apprenticeship and a
> practice so habitual that it has become instinctive. We must not be too
> ambitious. We cannot aspire to masterpieces. We may content our-
> selves with a joy ride in a paint-box. And for this, Audacity is the only
> ticket.

Art is not a profession which can be entered with assured prospects of
monetary gain, but when one really cares about what one is doing, money is
irrelevant compared with time and freedom for creative work. Some painters
never manage to achieve even a bare subsistence despite prodigious efforts,
a thought which seldom deters the dedicated individual. Artists want to be
allowed to work; money is not their primary objective, but they do need
and seek a basic security. In 1954 the American abstract painter Mark
Rothko, in despair at his plight, declared that if someone would pay him
$500 a month for the rest of his life, he would give them all his past work
and anything painted in the future. No one was prepared to accept this
offer. Yet, before he died in 1970, Rothko had become a major figure in
international art and his work sold for large sums.

Most painters would gladly exchange their entire yearly output for a
small but regular subsistence that would solve their financial worries. In
many countries the artist, because of the nature of his employment, is not
always included in the social benefits structure and receives neither sickness
pay nor retirement gratuities, let alone a weekly wage. The greatest single
advantage of the art profession is the fact that age is no barrier to the creative process. Artists often attain the peak of their powers in the twilight of
their lives.

Art is often a selfish pursuit that demands long, solitary periods of isolation which hinder social intercourse. With the exception of characters in

romantic novels, the artist seldom waits for inspiration or for the muse to lean on his shoulder. Half the battle of creativity in art is won by maintaining a strict working schedule. The productivity of the artist can be slowed by the interruptions of daily life which encroach upon his creative time. The greater the fame of the painter, the more difficulty he has in avoiding these intrusions. In many instances, painters have enjoyed long, formative years in quiet isolation that have allowed time for work and contemplation. Then they were 'discovered' and their way of life altered drastically. Fame demands a share of the artist's precious time. Success in art is a goal sought by all artists, yet when it is achieved it may be regarded as troublesome interference.

Professionalism in the arts is based upon total commitment to an ideal which occasionally borders on obsession. Creative art, more than any other occupation, stimulates personal expression, while allowing the fulfilment of idealistic values and granting the opportunity for a contribution to man's cultural heritage. In order to achieve his goal, the artist must continually persevere. When not actually engaged in working, he must enrich his mind to improve his art, but not even this dedication guarantees success. Many unforeseen obstacles lie on the long road to fulfilment. The act of creation must be its own reward and the artist must be prepared for criticism and rejection. A professional status in art lies not only in preparing exhibitions, making sales or winning praise from the critics, but also in demonstrating a strength of purpose resolute enough to overcome difficulties and obstructions.

ART EDUCATION AND STATE SUPPORT

ART SCHOOLS

Never before in history have there been as many artists as there are today. The competition is so great that only a fraction of them can hope to make a living entirely from the sale of their creative work. In spite of this fact, the ranks of eager students entering art schools continue to swell every year.

Many feel the desire to become artists, but relatively few actually stay the full course. Generally they tend to drop out after the first or second year of a four-year programme, some from disillusionment with art as a means of livelihood and others because they lack the necessary aptitude. Often those who graduate may fail to fulfil their potential.

Perhaps one of the most vexing questions asked of educational authorities today is 'Are art schools really necessary?' This query is generally based on the assumption that all talent in art is a gift and cannot be taught. The history of art is full of self-taught geniuses and therein lies the answer; for a young genius, formal school training is not a requisite, but for the vast majority, instruction and practice are the best means of attainment.

Students with natural artistic ability have a decided advantage, but if they fail to apply themselves, they can be overtaken by less naturally gifted fellows who are determined to succeed by sheer perseverance.

Art schools are often criticized for not instilling diligent working habits in their students. Indeed, some schools seem lax in allowing students to use the premises as a meeting-place for social contact or political agitation with applied study taking a secondary role. Graduates of these indulgent institutions often find they lack motivation to practice art on their own without the stimulus of daily assignments and the group atmosphere which the school had provided; consequently, they fall by the wayside and many give up art altogether. After four years in the comparative cocoon of an art school, often supported by student grants, they are simply not prepared for the reality of the working world. Although the school may have maintained a high standard of teaching proficiency, the student's most important assets remain a resolute inner discipline and a desire for creativity which supersedes all else.

Failure to have their training bear fruit is not entirely the fault of the students. In many instances schools provide laboratories and expensive equipment beyond the means of the individual. Graduation often brings an end to the student's right to use the school facilities. Deprived of his subsidy and the equipment essential to his work, the artist may feel quite cut off; he must either establish a private workshop and pay for its use or stop creating. In some areas artists have found an answer to this problem by opening workshops on a co-operative basis.

Having gone to an art school and earned a diploma does not automatically ensure proficiency, but it does imply a desire on the part of an individual to acquire a basic discipline in the profession.

TEACHING

Despite the numbers of students continually graduating from institutions as qualified art teachers, only a few find teaching situations which ideally suit them. Many of those who aspire to be fine artists drift into teaching merely as a means of supplementing their incomes. They find themselves as part-time staff at a school, and after a few years fall into a monotonous routine of supervising classes rather than instructing them. The fact that a person is a talented painter or sculptor does not automatically make him a good teacher with an ability to communicate to students. The age-old adage that teachers are born rather than made has more than a grain of truth.

Teaching requires an instinctive desire to communicate with students in a way that is both inspiring to them and fulfilling to the teacher. The ability to generate enthusiasm is a natural attribute that cannot really be taught.

Artists who have a particular aptitude for teaching sometimes discover that they gain as much as they give. They are able to expand their own theories by using the students as a sounding-board in a two-way dialogue. Students benefit enormously from inspired teaching. Some instructors who teach part-time are able to generate enthusiasm which might falter if they were required to lecture daily.

A few art school administrations are anxious to be thought of as progressive. They hire highly publicised painters to teach *avant garde* ideas to students who have not yet learned the basic fundamentals of art. Employing artists currently riding the crest of a fashionable wave may stimulate students for a time, but unless these artists have a basic dedication to teaching they soon lose interest and the students suffer. The great modern masters were thoroughly instructed in the classics before they progressed with new concepts in art. Picasso and Braque could draw a chair and table in perfect perspective before they abstracted them in cubistic planes. Art should be built on a firm foundation and the lessons of the past should not be ignored.

The early academies of art in the United States offered little more than tradition-bound art training based on drawing from the antique. However, with the growth of industrialisation in the middle of the nineteenth century, art was seen to be more closely allied with subjects of a technical nature such as architecture and engineering.

In recent years professional art schools have undertaken to incorporate scholarly academic subjects in their syllabuses to align more closely with university art departments. Mathematics, social studies, literature and psychology have been introduced to provide the art student with a more comprehensive education.

In the United States, where there are literally thousands of universities and training institutions as well as art schools, many art departments have been established on lines similar to the Old Masters' workshop organisation; the teacher presides as master while advanced students serve as assistants and guide less experienced students. The administration acts as the guild supplying materials and rules and regulations. This kind of harmonious relationship more often occurs in the areas of crafts and printmaking. Laboratory arts give wider scope for the novice who, after initial guidance, might happen upon new techniques which may be shared by others in the class.

An interesting aspect of the American educational scene is the appointment of important artists to posts in university art departments as artists-in-residence. Some of these appointees have been given prestigious commissions which the student body and faculty may be allowed to observe as the work progresses. Noted foreign artists who are invited through exchange programmes provide a new experience and stimulus for student artists.

An important development in art education in the United States, and now appearing increasingly in Great Britain, is the growth of university art galleries with well-organised exhibition programmes. Many of these are designed to generate interest for a wide audience and gain community support. Extension courses in various art subjects are widely offered. Both the university and the public are served by an increased appreciation and knowledge of the arts.

The tendency of American universities to concentrate on exhibiting and collecting has accelerated to the point that many museum administrations have found it necessary to compete not only for public attendance but also for prospective donors. Many collectors now look to the campus as the most likely centre to keep their collections intact and well-attended. This healthy competition has led several museum administrations to pull up their buttoned boots and reform lethargic and old-fashioned ways.

STATE SUPPORT

In the twentieth century patronage is provided by the State, philanthropical societies and industry as well as the private patron. The church and the great patrons are no longer a force. Private patronage is usually stimulated by the rising economy of a country. Many wealthy business organisations and institutions have adopted the role of patron and benefactor to the artist. Their patronage is not entirely motivated by altruistic ideals; it also has a publicity potential that is worthy of investment. Philanthropic commissions and grants that enable young artists to travel and study are perhaps the truest form of patronage, but even here bias may influence the selection of candidates.

Corporations that have formed large collections also sponsor exhibitions, give prizes and, perhaps more importantly, establish foundations and award scholarships. The competitive spirit that is so vital in business often extends to the promotion of art, with rival firms vying to build collections.

Industrial and philanthropical agencies in the United States are encouraged by tax benefits to commission works of art. Public art museums have received large collections as gifts through tax deductions.

Support of the arts at governmental level differs considerably from country to country. Yet it is significant that some form of recognition, whether it be financial or verbal, exists in nearly every nation in the world no matter how small or economically insignificant. Special provisions are often made by the governments of impoverished countries to promote their cultural heritage through performing and pictorial arts. These are sometimes proportionately in excess of many wealthier nations' contributions to the arts.

THE ARTIST IN SOCIETY

At the zenith of the great workshops, the artist had achieved a position of high esteem in society. In the early Middle Ages the actual manual labour involved in the creation of works of art resulted in the lower status of the art profession. The upper classes disdained any occupation that required the use of manual dexterity. The artist was regarded as a humble craftsman, sustained through comradeship in the guilds and by his religious convictions. During the Renaissance the artist achieved recognition by the state, church and persons of consequence. He was honoured as confidant and diplomatic emissary to reigning monarchs; he was further rewarded with knighthoods, given estates and the freedom of cities. Honorary degrees were bestowed upon him and he was entertained by cultivated international circles.

The artist could not rely entirely upon his creative talents to achieve for him an exalted position in life; he also had to be a person of intellect, able to discourse upon worldly subjects, with manners and attitudes befitting a gentleman of rank. Few artists fitted this role as perfectly as Rubens whose involvement in matters of state are renowned. Rubens thrived on the many diplomatic missions entrusted to him during his lifetime. He often acted as a courier to convey important negotiations between royal courts, travelling as an artist ostensibly to paint portraits.

Many notable painters attained privileged positions in the royal courts. Holbein, Raphael, van Eyck and Velasquez, among others, were appointed to posts of responsibility and diplomacy. The role of the painter as diplomat is without parallel today.

Several artists have gained lasting recognition for their writings on art rather than for their accomplishments as painters. These chroniclers wrote treatises on materials and techniques in contemporary use, biographies of artists and comments on the age in which they lived. Cennini, Van Mander, de Mayerne, Pliny, Theophilus, Vasari and Vitruvius are among the illustrious writers whose texts are essential reference sources for every art historian. In Cellini's famed autobiography, Leonardo's notebooks and Dürer's diary of his journey to the Netherlands were indelibly recorded for posterity. Important chroniclers of the nineteenth century include Eastlake, Laurie and Merrifield.

Letters written by artists have frequently provided missing pieces for reconstructing the jig-saw puzzles of their lives. The numerous letters of Rubens and Van Gogh indicate their desire to communicate with words as well as pictures. Rubens' command of languages and fluid writing style was enhanced by his ability to discourse on a variety of subjects. Van Gogh's letters to his brother Theo, although not literary gems, give us an intimate insight into the creation of particular paintings, his motivations and personal problems.

Many artists have felt compelled to comment on society, using their art as a manifestation of their feelings about war, crime, politics, social conditions and other injustices. A large volume of Goya's work exemplifies the horror and futility of war while Picasso, in a single painting, 'Guernica', spoke for the age in which we live. Visual chroniclers, such as Hogarth in England and Daumier in France, recorded daily life, human foibles, and the political atmosphere in witty or satirical drawings and engravings.

THE ARTIST IN LITERATURE AND FILMS

By the end of the eighteenth century, the artist came to be viewed in a new romantic light which was to change his status in society, as noted by Francis Haskell:

Formulated first in Germany and eventually adopted all over Europe as the romantic movement spread, this theory proclaimed that the artist was a genius whose very nature was, of necessity, different from and superior to that of the society in which he lived.

The artist has frequently been depicted as living in a garret and suffering untold hardships for his art. The opera *La Bohème* extols the virtues of the Bohemian existence for the romantically inclined. In reality, few artists have benefited aesthetically from dire poverty. Contrary to popular belief, hungry artists rarely produce great art. A great number of works have perhaps been lost to the world because their potential creators met an untimely end as a result of privation.

Rudyard Kipling's book *The Light that Failed*, first published in 1891 (a film version was made in 1939), presented the tragedy of an artist faced with impending blindness. Parallels with the popular conception of the artist as an ill-fated romantic figure can be found in several famous books and films in which fact has been liberally embroidered with fiction.

Three books based on the lives of great artists have been made into films. *Lust for Life*, by Irving Stone, portrayed the life of Vincent Van Gogh. In a memorable scene from the film, Van Gogh is shown painting at night wearing a hat with candles attached for illumination that demonstrated his intense creative desire. *The Agony and the Ecstasy*, also by author Irving Stone, re-created the Herculean labours of Michelangelo with the embellishment of the author's dialogue. In his famous fictional classic *The Moon and Sixpence*, Somerset Maugham presented Charles Strickland as the protagonist aping the life of Paul Gauguin. More than any true biographical work, this became generally accepted as an account of Gauguin's life.

A fictional work, *The Horse's Mouth* by Joyce Carey, gave life to a character named Gulley Jimson, who was meant to represent the lovable British eccentric as an artist. This book was also made into a film.

The turbulent lives of many artists have provided fascinating entertainment for countless readers and film-goers, and the legend that artists live on the brink of disaster continues to be perpetuated. There is a belief that great art justifies any bad behaviour on the part of its creator. The actions of a few of the most honoured artists of the past might prove quite reprehensible if they were observed today. Gauguin, for example, was an egotistical man who abandoned his family to become an artist. Seemingly incapable of warmth or human compassion, he used everyone for his own purposes. On the other hand, Renoir was sustained by close family relationships; but he is not exceptional, and many other artists also led normal, happily productive lives.

The public has been conditioned to assume that the life-style of an artist is quite remote from reality. The very word 'artist' conjures up a Bohemian character, flamboyantly attired and adopting a disdainful attitude towards the conventional way of life. Actually, the majority of successful artists think and dress very conventionally and are quite indistinguishable at a gathering—they might be bankers or clerical workers, from their appearance. It seems that only the consciously bizarre artists who frequent the cafés more than their studios invite attention.

The social privileges and esteem enjoyed by artists of renown in the past have largely disappeared, and the artist today is much less certain of himself and his status in the community. The position of artists during the Impressionist period was even more tenuous. Cézanne, now acknowledged as the father of modern painting, was virtually an outcast in his day. Although several modern painters have enjoyed publicity, wealth and good will, they are no longer accorded high governmental positions solely because of their fame in the world of art.

ART COLONIES

The founding of exclusive colonies where the artist can live and work amongst kindred souls apart from society is not a new aspect of the art scene. In the past, patrons commissioned or bought work directly from the artists, but with the decline of the workshop studios and the advent of art galleries and dealers, many painters preferred to move away from the city centres, often in the company of others in their profession. Most colonies were initially formed by a small group of truly dedicated artists who established the reputation of an area. Later, those on the fringe of the arts moved in, hoping the same aura of fame would surround them. The founding artists usually moved on when this occurred, leaving the colony to be inhabited by individuals in search of their own identities.

The fame of Barbizon was established by a nucleus of great French artists including Millet, Corot, Monet and Renoir. Pont Aven in Brittany was a favourite location of Paul Gauguin and grew to become a well-known colony. In Britain artists such as Barbara Hepworth and Ben Nicholson solidified their concepts and styles at St Ives in Cornwall.

In America art colonies have existed on the California coast at Carmel and Laguna Beach and amid the desert beauty of New Mexico at Taos and Santa Fe. Artists continue to migrate to natural beauty-spots and dwell together in communal groups of mutual sympathy and interest. Communal

living is a form of insulation against a possibly antagonistic outside world—
a protection the independent established artist no longer requires. Art
colonies, with their outward manifestations of flamboyant dress habits and
proliferating craft shops, have always served a purpose in the transition
from aspiring student to successful professional.

Mediterranean islands are particularly popular locations for art colonies.
Islands provide the perfect environment for those with escapist tendencies,
but they afford a universal problem for the artist who wishes to live apart
from society as he must seek out dealers and critics who are almost always
loath to travel. Only artists of international stature can afford to live in
remote regions outside the artistic perimeters and expect visits from the
connoisseurs.

Today art colonies are dotted about the world. The most famous have
international reputations, but one feature they all have in common is that
artists of repute usually avoid them as they would the plague.

MAKING A LIVING AS AN ARTIST

Perhaps the most vexing question asked of a budding artist is 'How are you
going to make a living?' This is an old cliché, familiar to every artist, which
does not have a satisfactory answer. A small proportion actually make a
living entirely from the sale of their work. Artists in this category are usually
internationally famous or regionally well-known. For most professionals,
though, life is a continual scramble of trying to make ends meet. In order
to secure a living for himself and his family, the artist is often forced to
compromise his idealistic dreams with practical reality. Before gaining the
time he requires for his art, the artist must first fulfil his commitments for
the necessities of lodging, food, clothing and sundries, as well as art
materials.

An artist whiling away the hours daubing at a canvas may seem to many
to have achieved the ideal life-style, but this impression of tranquillity can
be misleading. There is satisfaction for the soul, but often too little for the
body. There are no company pensions or sick pay, no paid holidays, no
weekly wages for long irregular hours. These drawbacks should be enough
to prevent gross over-population in the art profession.

The artist's chances of survival depend very much on his own initiative.
The ivory-tower attitude of working and waiting for the world to discover
him has ended the career of many an artist. A contemporary artist must
seize every opportunity to maintain his way of life, as competition is fierce.

Every avenue that may lead to new outlets for his artistic efforts must be explored. Art galleries in major cities are canvassed daily by a legion of artists hoping to be given the chance to exhibit. Even those who succeed in locating a gallery in which to show their work often find that they are out of pocket because sales have failed to match their expenses. In an art career discouragements are closer companions than triumphs.

The painter's world is one of constantly changing visual images. A face at a window, a tree bending in the wind, the light of a lamp—nothing is too fleeting to be captured and encapsulated in his memory for future reference. The artist may become an armchair traveller, like the primitive painter Rousseau, who was transported from his provincial cottage in France to the jungles of Africa on the wings of his imagination. Wild animals stalked his studio until he captured them on his canvases. When the painter stands in front of his canvas, he can cast off his mantle of obscurity and become once more totally absorbed by his fantasies.

It is little wonder that many artists find the irksome tasks of daily living an intrusion on the world of their imaginations. To be able to exist compatibly with society, the artist must adapt himself to worldly affairs. Art is a business and must be approached as any other capitalistic enterprise. Many artists of repute have risen to the pinnacle of their profession by a successful coalition of business acumen and sensitive vision.

One of the greatest assets an artist can have is a wife who believes in him and his work. The artist's earnings are often meagre and sporadic; wives who are dedicated to their husbands' careers make a vital contribution by taking jobs. A wife who is willing to endure hardships and disappointments on the long road to the fame that eludes most artists derives her pleasure and fulfilment from nurturing the creative spirit of her husband. Her attestation of faith is patronage in its most supreme, unselfish form.

Occasionally an artist is heard to say that he cannot bear to sell his pictures because they are his children. This generally implies an unprofessional status and may signify that no one has offered to buy them anyway. The truly dedicated painter's primary interest lies not in pictures he has completed, but in those on which he is currently at work and others he hopes to execute in the future. The painter must sell to live and the very act of achieving a sale signifies that he has communicated with another person.

The greater the amount an artist is able to earn from the sale of his pictures, the less time he must spend at endeavours unrelated to his art. The ultimate goal for most artists is financial independence derived entirely from selling their works.

OPEN EXHIBITIONS

A means of gaining recognition in the art world is by the submission of work to open exhibitions which are usually advertised in art journals. An artist whose work is accepted by the more important exhibitions is assured a certain amount of prestige and publicity as well as the possibility of sales.

In Great Britain the annual exhibitions of the various Royal Societies offer some of the best opportunities for public viewing. These shows are mainly supported by charging the artist an entry fee for his work and a hanging fee if it is accepted. Many contemporary artists consider open exhibitions like these to be riddled with anachronisms and never submit their pictures. There are seldom any cash awards offered, and for those rejected from the exhibition it means not only disappointment but a loss of time and money. The amateur painter is happy to exhibit anywhere he can, but the professional requires a greater potential return for his expenditure.

The vast numbers of amateurs submitting pictures to exhibitions have provided, on rare occasions, a lucrative operation for unscrupulous organisers. In a recent case, a nationally advertised exhibition was held in a provincial town for which a £3 entry fee was charged apart from the cost of shipping and pre-paid return. The so-called exhibition was held in a disused barn, the only expense to the organisers being a few mimeographed hand-sheets listing the artists' names and the titles of their works. The organisers made a profit of several hundred pounds.

One of the most important events on the London art calendar is the Royal Academy Exhibition. In an average year, 12,000 submissions are received from more than 4,000 artists. In spite of the entry fee, swarms of optimists arrive on 'sending-in day' on foot or by taxi, bicycle and van to join long queues at Burlington House; the majority of whom meet there again in equally long queues to collect their rejected work. The lucky entrant whose work is accepted receives a complimentary ticket for the season and an opportunity for his work to be seen by hundreds of potential buyers as well as dealers.

A sobering thought for the aspiring exhibitor to keep in mind is the amount of available space that is already allotted to predestined pictures as each Royal Academician is entitled to exhibit six works. The Academicians are usually reserved a hanging place 'on the line' at the viewer's eye level. In 1962, one-third of the exhibitors were members of the Royal Academy. Rejected artists are in good company. They may derive some consolation from the fact that the proportion of space remaining for unbiased selection is very small indeed when compared with the great number of pictures submitted.

In the United States open competitions and juried shows can actually become financial bonanzas for a few fortunate artists whose reputations are established. The same names often seem to win all the prizes—a fact which has not gone entirely unnoticed by critics. Although the artist is usually charged an entry fee, he does have a chance to win a cash or merchandise award and some of these can amount to substantial sums. The prizes are made available by the organisers who obtain the support of business firms and foundations that not only provide funds but often purchase works for their collections as well.

During the summer months, many cities and towns afford artists the opportunity to show in an outdoor setting. Outdoor exhibitions of paintings are generally thought to be of a low standard. Even those which are organised on an annual basis with juried entries are looked upon with disdain by gallery connoisseurs, although why paintings are any less acceptable when viewed in the open is something of a mystery. Were the same pictures to be exhibited in an established gallery, they would probably be accorded a better reception.

Outdoor sculpture exhibitions, on the other hand, are often given quite prestigious publicity. It seems that parks, recreational grounds and architectural backgrounds suit sculptural forms admirably. Changes of light and shade allow the viewer added attractions plus freedom to move about and discover new vantage-points. Henry Moore has said he prefers most of his work to be placed in open spaces.

PORTRAIT PAINTING

One of the most lucrative fields for an artist is painting portraits. If the painter has a particular talent or natural flair for obtaining a good likeness and is possessed of a pleasing social manner, he may well be lucky enough to secure a steady succession of sitters.

Portrait-painting is as old as art itself. The desire to have his countenance perpetuated in painting and sculpture is manifest in man. In the past, portrait artists enjoyed the company and often the friendship of the highest in the land, with all the attendant privileges. Portraits were in great demand at all levels of society, from the most wealthy personages to shopkeepers of modest means. No home was complete without paintings of immediate family members or ancestral portraits.

Unfortunately not all portrait painters were of Old Master calibre. Itinerant painters in England and in America roamed the countryside from village to village, painting signs for inns and shops while canvassing for potential portrait clients. They were generally untutored painters and some displayed only a modicum of natural ability. They often worked on canvases with previously painted backgrounds, and sometimes the figures themselves were painted in beforehand to speed the actual sittings. The artist had only to paint the face in the manner of the seaside photographer whose subjects stand with only their heads visible above cardboard figures.

The invention of the camera and photographic reproductions reduced many remaining sources of lucrative commissions in portraiture, illustration and copying which had previously occupied many artists. Deprived of a steady income, the artist soon became dependent upon dealers and galleries to find clients.

The demand for painted portraits declined; families no longer commissioned paintings to record their lineage and loved ones. The famous could now go to the photographer's salon where, in less than an hour, their likenesses were recorded for posterity, instead of spending valuable time sitting for an oil portrait.

In an article written in 1846 for the magazine *Living Age*, referring to the daguerreotype, it was stated:

> It is slowly accomplishing a great revolution in the morals of portrait painting. The flattery of the countenance delineators is notorious . . . Everybody who pays, must look handsome, intellectual, or interesting at least, on canvas. These abuses of the brush, the photographic art is happily designed to correct.

The fact that the camera cannot lie is probably the reason why portrait painting is once more becoming a force. Photography provided a new dimension for recording an exact likeness which was not always fully appreciated by the subject. Most mortals have an inherent desire to appear more handsome and interesting than they actually are in life.

A painter who specialises in portraits must be prepared to accept criticism from more than one source. Pleasing a sitter's family often becomes more important than pleasing the sitter. Everyone has a different idea of how the subject looks. One relative criticises the nose as being too long, another thinks the mouth is painted too wide, and so on. In the end, the portrait becomes a compromise between what the artist thinks it should be and the changes he must make to satisfy the family. The artist is seldom given licence to paint the subject just as he desires.

The pace of contemporary life has prevented many fine portrait artists from capturing a sitter's inner character; he must settle for an exterior resemblance, albeit a handsome picture. In less hurried days, kings and queens allotted a great deal of time to sit for their favourite painters, because they considered a handsome portrait as important an event as matters of state. Today an artist is fortunate indeed to have more than one hour or two with a head of state. Pietro Annigoni, who has been more privileged than most in being granted time to sketch Queen Elizabeth, has employed a model in his studio to represent the Queen wearing her royal robes and decorations.

Today a portrait artist is sometimes considered to be a dilettante who succeeds not by his ability as a painter but rather by his special connections with wealthy patrons. Most artists nowadays consider portraiture to be degradingly commercial. It may be that much of this jaundiced view is based on the inability of many contemporary artists to capture more than a superficial likeness of a subject. Failure to please a client has put an end to more than one artist's career in portrait painting.

Advertisements for genuine oil portraits copied from cherished photographs appear regularly in various publications. Despite the air of commercialism introduced into this field today, there still exists a small circle of eminent portrait painters whose work comes close to the great traditions of past masters. Modern artists, such as Graham Sutherland, Salvador Dali and others, have undertaken portrait commissions from time to time. Most famous modern artists are approached by hopeful sitters eager to have their portraits painted. In addition to the prestige of owning a portrait by a famous painter, it is likely that the painting will become historically as well as financially valuable. A good portrait painter is the pride of his bank manager, commanding fees beyond many artists' expectations.

EMPLOYMENT OPPORTUNITIES

The artist's ability to render an accurate likeness has been put to new uses by modern society. The public has become increasingly aware of the significant part artists play in sketching portraits of wanted criminals and missing persons. Frequently, the artist has little to work from other than descriptions by witnesses. A retentive memory and thorough anatomical

Page 143 'The Painter and the Connoisseur' by Pieter Bruegel the Elder, *c* 1565, in brown ink on paper. The painter is engaged in his work while a buyer fumbles for his purse

Page 144 (above) 'Louis XIV Visiting the Gobelins Factory' by Charles le Brun, a tapestry, 1663–75. (below) Henry Moore in his studio working on an etching plate of an elephant's skull

knowledge is required for this specialised work. The Identi-kit composite picture file evolved from the artist's memory sketch.

A descendant of Sir Joshua Reynolds, artist Roy Reynolds, figured prominently in a case involving an unidentified murdered woman. Previously Mr Reynolds had demonstrated a remarkable ability to draw the characteristic features of unidentified attackers from descriptions given him by their victims. His portraits were instrumental in the apprehension of a number of criminals by the police. In this instance, the police asked Mr Reynolds if he could draw a portrait from the dead woman's skull. After taking careful measurements and making several preliminary sketches, he produced a drawing which was circulated by the news media and eventually led to the identification of the murdered woman.

Another absorbing and specialised art career is that of medical illustrator which requires some training in medicine and a particular aptitude for the subject. Fine artists with more than average skill and interest in anatomical illustration may find satisfaction in this field.

There are an increasing number of career opportunities within the field of art, apart from teaching. Advertising, industrial design, architectural rendering, film animation, interior design, book illustration, art restoration and picture framing are among many occupations open to artists.

PAINTING FOR REPRODUCTION

Easel paintings are becoming increasingly accepted in the publishing business as the gap between fine art and advertising art diminishes. Credit for this phenomenon is due to the astounding success of Pop Art, which derives from commercial art and emerged as a force in the 1960s. Reproductions of fine art paintings and graphics are seen by editors as giving a certain 'tone' to their publications.

Painters may either sell their original works to the publisher or merely grant permission for their reproduction, and in either case the copyright ordinarily remain the painter's. In either case, the artist should ask a fee for reproduction rights commensurate with the price of the work. There are no fixed rules regarding reproduction fees; they may range from 10 per cent to 100 per cent of the value of the illustration. However, the artist should take into consideration the additional publicity he will receive from this exposure and fix his price accordingly.

Some painters adapt their style and subject-matter specifically for the reproduction market. They generally work under contract for firms specialising in fine-art reproductions for the trade. Payment may be in the form of an agreed sum outright, or royalties based on the sales of the reproductions similar to those made to authors of books. The latter arrangement is the more exciting; if the art reproduction becomes a bestseller, the artist stands to make considerably more than he would from a single final payment. Tretchikoff, the famous master of painting reproductions, has amassed a considerable fortune through the success of a few outstanding prints such as the 'Chinese Girl', of which several hundred thousand copies have been sold.

The English painter David Shepherd is another celebrated reproduction artist whose pictures of wild life in general and elephants in particular have earned him a rich and secure living. Shepherd's success in painting animals follows a precedent set by Sir Edwin Landseer, reproductions of whose 'The Monarch of the Glen' and 'Stag at Bay' adorned the walls of almost every home in Victorian England.

Every country has its favourite reproductions. In America one of the most popular prints found in middle-class homes some years ago depicted an Indian in a slumped position on horseback entitled 'The End of the Trail' or 'The Dying Indian'. Another popular print, 'September Morn', showed a nude girl modestly standing ankle-deep in a lake beside some rocks. This print was used for many years to advertise a well-known brand of whisky. Today the popular reproduction images are more likely to be Andy Warhol's Marilyn Monroe series or Robert Indiana's American flags.

Colour reproduction processes were once a laborious undertaking. Mezzotint engravers and etchers were employed to painstakingly copy popular paintings on to metal plates, making a separate plate for every colour. Each plate had to be inked and printed individually—a time-consuming operation. Photographic reproduction methods and machinery capable of producing thousands of copies a day have replaced the old hand techniques of printing. Not only are the reproductions faithful to the original in detail, but the thickness of the original paint layers may even be imitated by a special process.

STUDIO SALES AND CO-OPERATIVES

An artist without gallery affiliations is free to conduct his affairs according to his own inclinations; however, he must be prepared to arrange appointments with viewers to visit his studio. This invasion results in a loss of privacy, but most of all it absorbs great periods of creative time and energy.

The value of gallery representation is realised after a procession of prospective purchasers has rummaged through the studio, seeking pictures with 'just the right colours' to match home furnishings or, equally distasteful, has tried to haggle with the artist over his quoted prices. Studio sales have only one obvious advantage—the artist does not have to share his earnings with a gallery.

Artists without gallery attachments and those disillusioned with the gallery system have sometimes banded together to form co-operatives for their mutual benefit. The members pool their resources to rent gallery space and then establish an exhibition policy. Three or four artists may be selected as a board of directors and given power to make decisions for the whole group. In some instances the artists have hired a manager to run the gallery on their behalf. One-man exhibitions are scheduled on a rotation basis. Each exhibitor must assume responsibility for gallery and publicity expenses during the course of his exhibition. Ideally, a co-operative association limits the number of members so that the intervals between each individual's exhibitions are not too long.

Co-operative galleries have generally had little appeal in Great Britain where artists have traditionally worked independently. The possible exceptions are a few small but historically important movements such as the Pre-Raphaelites, the Vorticists and the Camden Town Group.

In New York recently a number of well-known artists decided to sever their connections with their galleries in order to become more independent and to avoid the exorbitant commissions being asked—in many cases up to 50 per cent. The artists felt that they would soon be economically forced to abandon painting if this trend continued. Rather than submit to further indignities, the artists opened their own studio-galleries in warehouses in lower-rent districts to deal directly with potential buyers, thus eliminating both the dealer and his commission. The temperaments of some of the artists were simply not suited to this kind of public exposure and ultimately they decided that it was better for a dealer to handle their affairs and they returned to the gallery system. Other artists enjoyed the direct contact with clients and increased their earnings substantially.

MORE PLACES TO EXHIBIT

Art galleries are not the only locations where one may exhibit. The premises of many types of businesses afford an amenable atmosphere where art may be displayed to a varied audience. Banks, libraries, bookshops, department stores, antique shops, and theatre clubs are all prospective exhibition sites. As these establishments are not normally engaged in the sale of art, they will probably ask a smaller commission on sales than would a gallery.

Architects, interior decorators and other professions allied with art are often disposed to holding exhibitions; an enterprising firm may even set aside a room in their offices for this purpose. Architects and interior decorators are frequently commissioned by clients to select works of art which complement their designs for homes and offices.

Museums offer another venue for the artist. Although most museum exhibitions are organised by arts councils, many museums are receptive to enquiries from individual artists to augment their exhibition programmes. Museums do not attempt to sell or compete with private galleries on a business basis. Although sales may not be readily forthcoming, a museum exhibition has considerable prestige value.

BARTERING

In the past, artists had some success in exchanging works of art for food, clothing, medical services and various other necessities. Trading in kind is not as prevalent today, but it is a means of avoiding either a cash expenditure or receiving a taxable payment for works sold. Instances of bartering have been recorded by some of the greatest artists of history.

During a visit to Antwerp in 1520 Dürer wrote:

> Stephen Capelle [a goldsmith] has given me a cedarwood rosary, for which I promise to take, and have taken his portrait. I bought some furnace-brown and pair of snuffers for 4 st. I paid 3 st. for paper. I made a pen-and-ink portrait in his book of Felix kneeling. He gave me 100 oysters.

One only hopes Dürer was fond of oysters.

In another instance, Dürer wrote: 'I dined with the Treasurer, Herr Lorenz Sterk; he gave me an ivory whistle and a very pretty piece of porcelain, so I gave him a whole set of prints.' It would seem that with current prices, at least, Herr Sterk had the best of this bargain.

Trading pictures for painting materials has sometimes been a beneficial arrangement for both the artist and the vendor. Père Tanguy's trading of art supplies for paintings by Cézanne and Van Gogh is an example. It is unlikely that a painter approaching a supplier of art materials today would be accorded such an exchange. A painter in London recently enquired of the largest firm of art suppliers how much of a discount they offered to professionals, and was told, 'None at all! There is no need since we have more than enough amateur trade to keep us in business.'

INCOME TAX

An annual and unavoidable event on the artist's calendar is the preparation of income tax statements. The majority of fine artists fall into the self-employed bracket which usually requires complex tax forms.

An artist's income may be derived either from the sale of his work or from fees, wages or commissions. He is subject to the usual tax conditions imposed upon any self-employed person. Perhaps the only difference between artists and others engaged in running their own businesses is that artists are sometimes remiss in matters of bookkeeping and accounts. If the artist is a professional earning the greater proportion of his income in this field, he will be best advised to seek the services of an accountant who can offer guidance.

The artist may not be cognisant of certain tax concessions; for example, a scheme to average out the artist's fluctuating income over a period of several years is operated in some countries. An artist may declare a room in his home as his studio and place of work and a deduction may be made in proportion to his rent or mortgage payments. In Great Britain artists can no longer claim entertaining expenses for prospective customers and dealers, but in the United States this practice is still applicable. A deduction may be permitted for travel which may include short journeys to galleries for picture delivery or more extensive travel abroad either in connection with exhibitions or for painting purposes.

A record of all sales must be kept to verify earnings for the year; any supplementary income from other sources must also be reported. Expenditure on paints, canvases, frames and other materials should be listed as deductions; therefore it is necessary to obtain and keep any receipts for professional expenditures either of a material nature or for services rendered. The hiring of models and the photographing of paintings may be allowable deductions.

CHAPTER 11

GALLERIES

ESTABLISHING A GALLERY

The establishment of a successful art gallery requires something more than the desire to be associated with cultural endeavours. Anyone can hang a sign advertising himself as a dealer or art connoisseur. Gallery owners come from varied backgrounds; ideally, their previous experience should have been in the related fields of art or selling. Some have been artists themselves but realised their abilities for organisation surpassed their talents as painters. An aptitude for public relations is useful and sound financial backing is indispensable. A collector who delights in selling or trading items from his collection may become a successful dealer; indeed many collectors have entered the trade this way.

The purpose of a gallery is to serve as a shop window for the exhibition and sale of works of art. The dealer's function is to promote the status of the artist and to negotiate transactions on his behalf, leaving the artist free for his creative pursuits. To accomplish this and make a profit requires hours of time and dedication outside the normal working day.

Organising the daily routine of a gallery includes preparing for exhibitions, arranging for advertising and publicity, printing and mailing invitations and catalogues, answering telephone or postal queries, advising artists and clients, settling accounts and, above all, the pleasurable but time-consuming task of viewing art work. The director's activities may include attending exhibitions to search for new talent and buying at auctions. A certain portion of his time is spent entertaining and being entertained.

The location of the gallery is of paramount importance; most tend to congregate in close proximity to one another. The more elegant galleries are usually situated in the most fashionable shopping area, often along one particular street. Clients, critics, potential customers, in fact everyone interested in art finds it more convenient and stimulating to be able to visit several galleries in a single journey. Smaller galleries form on the perimeter, in lower-rent premises, hoping eventually to move into the select street. A few attempt to break new ground in suburban surroundings where overheads are minimal by comparison, but where isolation can be restrictive to success.

The premises of many art galleries are converted business establishments which formerly housed a variety of trades and products. Conversions may be expensively elaborate or surprisingly simple. The minimum essentials for a gallery need be no more than adequate lighting and hanging arrangements, storage space, a desk and a telephone. Besides rent, the principal initial outlay is for a secretary/receptionist. As the gallery prospers, expenses will increase—but after all, what other business is supplied with completely free stock?

Modern galleries which specialise in exhibiting the works of living artists occasionally supplement their income by buying and selling period pictures. Various schemes may be introduced to help keep a gallery solvent. As it is in the artist's interest that his showplace remains open, he should be willing to co-operate in most new ventures. Renting paintings, for example, is one means of attracting new clients to the gallery. A number of those who rent pictures for limited periods find they want to keep them; the rental fee is then usually applied to the purchase price. It is fairly common practice for a gallery to allow regular clients to take paintings home on approval.

A constant hazard of gallery ownership is the possibility of theft. Although numerous security devices are available, they are expensive and most are operative only when the gallery is closed. A great many thefts occur during business hours; deceiving or distracting staff members is the usual method employed to steal works of art. Insurance coverage is standard procedure with galleries but it is not always a certainty; artists should enquire if their works on the premises are covered.

FINDING A GALLERY

A problem that faces every artist at one time or another is that of finding a gallery. The necessity of gallery affiliation is often questioned, but for those who have been rejected, the answer is painfully clear. An artist without gallery representation feels hopelessly adrift and isolated in an unsympathetic world. Even the painter who succeeds in selling his own work almost always suffers from lack of a wider recognition of his talent.

The search for a gallery can be approached systematically. Every large art-conscious metropolis has a trade newspaper or journal which lists all the city's galleries and exhibitions. An artist who wants to save time would be wise to consult a knowledgeable painter or art enthusiast to determine which galleries might be most likely to find his work of interest. In New York, for example, there are more than four hundred private galleries, while in London there are about three hundred. This presents a daunting prospect; probably 90 per cent of these galleries might not be interested in the works of an unknown artist because nearly all specialise in different schools or periods of painting. Some galleries never exhibit the work of living artists. These range from galleries that show top-quality Old Masters or Impressionists to those that stock sporting prints and paintings, Victoriana and other items.

Modern galleries that exhibit the work of living artists may handle only Pop, Op, Hard-edge or Constructivist work. One gallery shows Surrealists, another Primitives and most of them would rarely introduce a new painter into their limited stable, especially one 'off the street'.

It is futile to start enquiries with the most important galleries—a brisk rebuff is almost assured. Top-ranking galleries in New York, London and Paris have as many as one hundred artists a week approaching them. It is better to begin with less high-powered dealers who may have a little more time and interest in seeing new work. Once an artist becomes successful with a small gallery, the larger galleries may become interested in his work. It is always helpful for an artist to have an introduction or recommendation to the gallery under consideration, although an artist with a really outstanding portfolio, or an extensive professional background, may be accepted without this formality.

The artist is advised to make a preliminary appointment before visiting a gallery with his work. A telephone call will ascertain when it is convenient for the director to view paintings and will ensure the artist a cordial reception. Some directors set aside certain hours during the week for interviews. Many a naïve artist has made the mistake of walking in unannounced, portfolio in hand. Should he inadvertently commit the cardinal sin of interrupting a potential sales discussion between the director and a client, he will not endear himself to the gallery.

Gallery directors are usually not prepared to discuss requests for one-man shows during preliminary conversations with an artist; he would be better advised to seek inclusion in a group show. This gives the director an option to show a few pictures in order to assess his clients' reactions without committing himself more deeply.

RISKS TO THE ARTIST

Newly established galleries in out-of-the-way locales are sometimes a gamble, but for an artist trying to establish himself, these present greater opportunities for exhibitions. A new dealer will still be formulating his ideas and is more receptive to meeting and talking with artists before he has established his policy. If the gallery prospers, the dealer may decide to move to a more central location, taking his artists with him.

A small number of galleries exist that profit almost exclusively from selling exhibition space to artists from out of town or abroad. Young students and amateur painters from all walks of life are the principal exhibitors, but occasionally arrangements are made with foreign galleries to exhibit the work of more experienced artists. Only a few of these shows are successful, as the policy of these pay-to-exhibit galleries is well known to critics and collectors.

The artist should tread warily in his search for a suitable gallery. There are dealers who open a gallery for little purpose other than to give themselves a veneer of respectability as art patrons. They take little interest in the practical business of running a gallery and often opt out of their responsibilities to the artist. Fortunately, this type of dealer is a rare exception as running a gallery is a full-time occupation.

While most reputable galleries make their profits from the sale of pictures, some attempt to cover their costs through the artist. Not only is the artist expected to pay all expenses, but the gallery relies upon him to invite his own circle of friends to the exhibition. The dealer, in this instance, has no great incentive to promote sales as his overheads have already been financed by the artist.

It is unfortunate that the artist is often among the last to hear that a gallery with which he is associated is going out of business. Some galleries simply close and the artist is left to trace the whereabouts of his work afterwards. An even less desirable situation arises when a gallery goes bankrupt. Legal complications could impound his consigned work for months and it is possible for outstanding creditors, under certain circumstances, to have the work sold in order to reimburse their losses.

Engaging in the art profession is a calculated risk; unless it is taken, the

10

artist has little hope of succeeding. Trust is the operative word, but the onus is on the artist who must rely on the integrity of the dealer to settle his accounts and to return his work safely.

ART SERVICES

The problem of finding a gallery and clients has been considerably reduced by enterprising art services whose function is to fill the gap between the artist and his audience. This type of service is rapidly expanding in several major art centres. The service provides a central location in which information pertinent to the art profession is housed and correlated. In a sense these organisations might be considered as the modern equivalent of the guilds.

The Art Information Centre Inc of New York City is a large non-profit organisation established to liaise with artists, dealers, collectors and institutions. In addition, it gives assistance to those wishing to locate the work of any living artist. The centre maintains close contact with galleries, schools, business firms, groups and individuals associated with the arts. The reference index contains many categories and styles ranging from oil paintings to multiples and three-dimensional wall pieces. On file are the monographs of hundreds of artists together with photographic examples of their work. The service will undertake the co-ordination of sales or commissions between a prospective client and an artist or simply establish the contact. Gallery directors use the service to find new talent; artists are advised on which galleries might be interested in their work.

In Great Britain the Art Information Registry Ltd maintains a visual library of 35mm transparencies together with biographical and general documentation on the work of professional artists. This organisation offers the same basic service as its American counterpart, but clients other than artists are charged a consultancy fee. A technical register is available for artists who have enquiries regarding insurance, legal matters, transport, art material suppliers, award schemes and directories on cultural organisations.

In Britain the artist is offered a wider selection of galleries to contact than ever before. Whereas it was once mandatory to exhibit in London in order to achieve recognition, the decentralisation of art galleries in the late 1950s has resulted in a mushrooming of new showplaces in the provinces.

GALLERY COMMISSIONS

Galleries rarely purchase works outright; they usually take them on consignment for sale or return. They operate on a percentage basis, taking 25–50 per cent. Most galleries take $33\frac{1}{3}$ per cent, so that a gallery asking 50 per cent must do a good deal for the artist to justify this sum. Work taken on consignment should always be insured and protected while in the gallery; however, some galleries do not accept this responsibility and it is left to the artist to sustain any loss or damage.

An artist connected with a gallery may occasionally be asked to allow a client to visit his studio to view a larger selection of his paintings. In this event, the gallery will probably ask for a commission of approximately 10–20 per cent of any resulting sales in deference to the artist having to bear the burden of negotiating with the client.

PRICING

The price an artist charges for his work is relative to many factors. The amount charged should be related to his professional experience. If he has exhibited before, a precedent is established. If not, the dealer will probably suggest a mutually agreed price range based on the dealer's knowledge of the current market. Another factor to be considered is the varying sizes of pictures; a large painting usually commands a greater sum than a small one. Yet, quality is all-important and a fine picture of small dimension may equal or exceed the price of a larger work.

Some galleries ask the artist to quote the sum he wishes to receive for his paintings. This gives a dishonest dealer room to operate a scale of prices according to the size of his client's purse. Works are often marked up more than 200 per cent from the artist's price. The artist is rarely given a share of this excess profit. If the dealer buys a picture outright, he is free to bargain, but if the work is on consignment, the artist should insist on a proper commission arrangement. Prohibitive prices can greatly reduce the opportunity for further sales. Occasionally, a buyer discovers he has been overcharged and blames the innocent artist along with the unscrupulous dealer.

In the case of multiple original graphics, the artist should always set the retail price so that other prints from the edition will be uniformly priced in each gallery to which they are consigned. Variation is bound to reflect upon both the artist and the dealer. Again, if a dealer purchases the prints outright, the artist no longer has control over the price, but at least he is no longer ethically responsible for the dealer's actions.

Galleries prefer to hang oils, watercolours and prints, rather than drawings. Wall space is at a premium and drawings represent less profit margin. The advantage of displaying prints is that because of their multiple nature more than a single sale can result, perhaps ultimately totalling amounts greater than those of oil paintings. Drawings are often shown during sculpture exhibitions, as there is wall space to be filled behind the work displayed on the floor.

Discounts on works of art ranging from 10 per cent to 20 per cent may be considered; museums and educational institutions are normally granted this concession. Purchasers who order in large quantities and well-known collectors are sometimes accorded a discount as well. Galleries do not offer discounts too freely lest they lose their reputations for fair and stable prices. Any discount offered should be with the full consent of the artist. Some galleries allow clients to pay by instalments; artists may find that payment for these sales is often a long time forthcoming, since their accounts are not normally settled until the buyer has paid the gallery for his purchase. Some galleries pay the artist immediately after receipt, others pay quarterly or annually. A few settle accounts only after repeated requests by the artist.

Galleries can obtain astonishingly high prices for decoratively fashionable works. A selling artist is treated as a red-hot show-biz investment by his gallery director who is quick to ride on the bandwagon with his protégé; however, a painter whose fame rises meteorically may find it can diminish with equal rapidity.

ONE-MAN SHOWS

Before a one-man show takes place the gallery may ask the artist to sign a binding contract stipulating the responsibilities to be agreed upon by both parties. The form of this contract may vary with the location of the gallery and the policy of the director. Contractual terms may stipulate the exhibition dates, the amount of gallery commission, the division of exhibition expenses, the gallery's responsibilities towards promotion, the disposition of works left on consignment and various other related matters.

Some contracts may appear extremely restrictive. Apart from a disproportionate amount of expense and responsibility for the artist, a clause may be inserted preventing him from exhibiting with another gallery for a year before and after the exhibition dates. Such a stipulation is deplorable, although it may be reasonable for a gallery to request exclusive rights for a three- or four-month period following the exhibition. The artist should weigh the consequences before signing a contract which binds or restricts him professionally for any lengthy period.

One form of agreement covering exhibitions allows for a set amount to cover gallery expenses. The artist is liable for this fee whether anything is sold or not. It may be agreed that the sum requested from the artist should be made up by the dealer choosing unsold pictures from the exhibition in lieu of cash.

Important galleries may offer certain artists in their stable an annual stipend to cover living expenses. In return the gallery takes a large proportion of the artist's production. Some designate a specific number of square feet of painted surface area that the artist is expected to cover during the year in order to fulfil his contract, although he may vary the size of his paintings as he wishes.

Written contracts are the exception rather than the rule. Usually, a gallery requires no more than a verbal gentleman's agreement to plan a show. However, through a contract, the artist is made fully aware of the conditions as set forth and the gallery is protected from any misunderstanding which may arise. Compromise and equality in sharing expenses and profits are the best policies for a lasting gallery relationship.

Arrangements for one-man shows must be made well in advance of the proposed date of opening. Gallery exhibition programmes are sometimes fixed as much as two years in advance. However, through unforeseen circumstances, a vacancy may occur in the calendar permitting one artist to present an exhibition in place of another.

One of the most important functions that the artist and gallery director share is choosing the work to be shown in a one-man show. Almost invariably, the director wants the painter's work to be uniformly consistent in style. Eclecticism is frowned upon; the painter's style must be as easily identifiable as his handwriting. Other preparations for the show may include pricing the paintings, having photographs made for the catalogue or publicity, providing biographical material, framing the pictures and transporting them to the gallery.

Holding a one-man show is always a time of trepidation for both the painter and the gallery director, and while the exhibition is in progress both are vitally concerned about the eventuality of sales and the critics' reviews. If the show is not a success the dealer can at least look forward to his next exhibition. For the artist, it is a different story. He has not only failed to recoup his expenses but is out of pocket for all his time as well. It may be some years before he can prepare another show.

The occasion of a one-man show conjures up wondrous possibilities of sales for an artist. No situation can be more desirable than that of an exhibition which has sold out. The gallery is then in the enviable position of establishing a waiting list of clients eager to secure a painting by the artist in demand.

Openings attended by friends of the artist and the gallery often provide the best opportunities for sales, but they may be the only ones which occur during the course of the exhibition. Dealers sometimes wage psychological warfare in order to promote buying; when sales flag, more than one gallery director has been known to affix red 'sold' dots as a spur to stimulate buying.

A gallery with sufficient space is wise to keep an exhibition in storage for a week or two following its closure as the end of an exhibition does not necessarily mean the termination of sales. A profusion of red dots cannot help but give an artist a feeling of confidence. Success in selling may not be the principal goal of a dedicated artist, but it certainly comes second.

In a sense, a painter is always preparing for an exhibition, but when a date has actually been fixed, he is imbued with a greater feeling of commitment and urgency. It acts as a stimulus to his creativity and gives him a heightened awareness that his work will soon be seen publicly and judged on its merits. Presenting a one-man show is the moment of truth for a painter. It should reveal to him immediately any weaknesses or discrepancies in his work; paintings seen for the first time in a gallery environment take on new meanings and implications for the artist. A one-man exhibition often acts as a milestone in the painter's evolution. For many it polarises the work of the past and plants the seed of inspiration for the future.

PRIVATE VIEWS

The opening of an exhibition is usually heralded with a private view attended by friends, critics, celebrities and potential buyers. The artist can frequently be spotted as the person who appears the most ill-at-ease.

The gallery mailing list is compiled from many sources and is added to after every exhibition. 'Signing the book' is a ritual observed at most private views. From this register, the gallery selects likely clients who may be interested in future exhibitions. Many élite galleries keep exacting records of their clients' special interests and preferences in pictures.

It is not obligatory to hold a private view, and a great many successful exhibitions open without them; however, the added expense is often justified by increased sales and the good will that is generated.

PRIVATE DEALERS [AND [AGENTS

A number of private fine art dealers conduct their operations from their homes, independent of galleries. They benefit by not having expensive gallery overheads and regular exhibitions to prepare. Clients may visit a dealer's home or office where the work may be seen in a private environment instead of the rather artificial surroundings of a gallery. An easier and more personal rapport between dealer and client may develop in this atmosphere. Dealers may advertise their services 'By appointment only', but usually they build a clientele through personal associations. They act as advisers to clients, offer counsel to their artists and occasionally provide moral and financial support to particularly gifted protégés. Dealers are scouts always looking for new talent. Although private dealers may not have galleries, they may arrange exhibitions through their contacts for the artists they are promoting.

A dealer may sometimes assume that the artist is not the best judge of his own work and he may try to influence him to alter his style or change his subject-matter. Enlightened dealers believe in educating the public to understand and appreciate the artist's work instead of trying to influence him in any way. The best relationship between the artist and dealer is one of mutual confidence.

An art agent differs from a fine art dealer mainly by the nature of the art he promotes and the contacts he pursues. The agent usually represents freelance commercial illustrators, but will occasionally accept a few fine artists as clients since easel paintings are in vogue for magazine illustrations. Normally, an agent makes the rounds of the publishing houses selling finished works or the rights to reproduce, or securing commissions. Those who represent fine artists will visit galleries, public institutions and recommended contacts. Some agents charge a fee for their services, others only a commission on the work they sell.

It is wise to be wary of a dealer or agent who promises to open the doors of the art world for a budding artist upon payment of a fee. Reputable art agents generally earn their living by taking an agreed commission from sales, not by charging the artist an initial sum or by the hour.

Some firms employ agents to promote various schemes to attract buyers and open new markets. One method of bringing art before the public is by office-to-office canvassing, a variation of the door-to-door approach. A few enterprising salesmen take art to the householder by vans equipped for hanging pictures—virtually galleries on wheels. In the United States a firm of publishers of original prints has a fleet of vans which tour from city to city exhibiting at colleges and universities. They reach a large audience of young potential collectors who may have limited means but who can afford to buy prints.

At one time, dealers made and broke reputations; it took as much as eight to ten years to build an artist's name. Today, with mass media, the same process may take only two or three years.

BIBLIOGRAPHY

GENERAL

Churchill, Sir Winston. *Painting as a Pastime*. London: Penguin Books, 1964. Reprinted from W. Churchill's *Thoughts and Adventures*. London: Thornton Butterworth, 1932

Elsen, Albert E. *Purposes of Art*. New York: Holt, Rinehart & Winston, 1967

Murray, Peter and Linda. *Dictionary of Art and Artists*. London: Thames & Hudson, 1965

GENERAL ART HISTORY

Antal, Frederick. *Florentine Painting and Its Social Background*. London: Kegan Paul, 1948

Christensen, Erwin O. *The History of Western Art* (paperback). New York: New American Library, 1959

Gardner, Helen. *Art through the Ages*. New York: Harcourt, Brace & World, 1959

Gombrich, E. H. *The Story of Art*. New York: Phaidon, 1950

Levey, Michael. *A Concise History of Painting*. New York: Praeger, 1962

Newton, Eric. *The Arts of Man*. Greenwich, Conn: New York Graphic Society, 1960

Orpen, Sir William (ed). *The Outline of Art*. Revised by Horace Shipp. London: George Newnes, 1957

PREHISTORIC

Moulin, Raoul-Jean. *Prehistoric Painting*. Trans Anthony Rhodes. London: Heron Books, 1966

THE ANCIENT WORLD

Boardman, John. *Greek Art*. New York: Praeger, 1964

Boulanger, Robert. *Egyptian Painting and the Ancient East*. Trans Anthony Rhodes. London: Heron Books, 1966

Gassiot-Talabot, Gérald. *Roman and Palaeo-Christian Painting*. Trans Anthony Rhodes. London: Heron Books, 1966

Pliny's Chapters on the History of Art. Ed and trans K. Jex-Blake and Eugene Sellers-Strong. Chicago: Argonaut, 1968. A modern adaptation of Pliny's celebrated treatise

Spiteris, Tony. *Greek and Etruscan Painting*. Translated by Janet Sondheimer. London: Heron Books, 1966

MEDIEVAL

Conway, Sir Martin. *The Van Eycks and Their Followers*. London: John Murray, 1921. A rewritten and extended version of his previous book *Early Flemish Artists*. Chapter VIII is about the guild system

Conway, William Martin. *Literary Remains of Albrecht Dürer*. Cambridge: Cambridge University Press, 1889. A translation of the writings of Albrecht Dürer including his famous *Diary of a Journey to the Netherlands* and letters to patrons and friends.

Elst, Van Der, Joseph, Baron. *The Last Flowering of the Middle Ages*. New York: Doubleday, Doran, 1944. A most readable book about Flemish artists and the important centres of Flemish painting during the Middle Ages. Chapter V contains an excellent description of the medieval guilds

Herubel, Michel. *Gothic Painting*, Vols I–II. London: Heron Books, 1966

Levey, Michael. *Dürer*. London: Weidenfeld & Nicholson, 1964

Peers, Mrs C. R. *The Early Northern Painters*. London: Medici Society, 1922

Renard, Georges. *Guilds in the Middle Ages*. London: G. Bell, 1918. New York: republished by A. M. Kelley, 1968. Contains an important edited introduction by G. D. H. Cole on the history of the English guilds

Staley, Edgcumbe. *The Guilds of Florence*. London: Methuen, 1906. A comprehensive study with many translations from actual surviving documents. Chapter VIII is particularly relevant for painters

Whinney, Margaret. *Early Flemish Painting*. London: Faber & Faber, 1968. A survey of the principal artists of medieval painting

THE OLD MASTERS

Avermaete, Roger. *Rubens and His Times*. London: George Allen & Unwin, 1968. Trans from the French, *Rubens et Son Temps*

Cellini, Benvenuto. *The Autobiography of Benvenuto Cellini*. Trans by J. A. Symonds. New York: Doubleday, 1948

Clark, Kenneth. *Leonardo Da Vinci*. Cambridge: Cambridge University Press, 1952

Egan, Patricia. *Raphael*. London: Harry N. Abrams, 1960

Magurn, Ruth Saunders. *The Letters of Peter Paul Rubens*. Cambridge, Mass: Harvard University Press, 1955

Mander, Carel van. *Dutch and Flemish Painters*. Translation from the Schilderboeck and introduction by Constant van de Wall. New York: McFarlane, Warde, McFarlane, 1936. Carel van Mander was a sixteenth-century painter and chronicler of artists in the low countries

Seymour, Charles, Jr. *The Sculpture of Verrocchio*. London: Studio Vista, 1971. An account of Verrocchio's working life

Vasari, Giorgio. *Vasari's Lives of the Artists*. Abridged and edited by Betty Burroughs. London: Allen & Unwin, 1960. The biographies of the most eminent architects, painters and sculptors of Italy. A vital reference source for almost every modern biographer

White, Christopher. *Rubens and His World*. London: Thames & Hudson, 1968

THE MODERN MOVEMENT

Renoir, Jean. *Renoir My Father*. Trans Randolph and Dorothy Weaver. London: Collins, 1962. An intimate account of the artist's life and family.

Rewald, John. *The History of Impressionism*. New York: Modern Museum of Art, 1946

MATERIALS AND METHODS

Cennini, Cennino d'Andrea. *The Craftsman's Handbook*. Yale University Press, 1933. Republished by Dover. English trans by D. V. Thompson of Yale University Press's *Il Libro dell'Arte* published in 1933. The famous early fifteenth-century Florentine treatise on medieval painting which reveals many recipes and techniques

Constable, W. G. *The Painter's Workshop*. London: Oxford University

Press, 1954. A most excellent book about the organisation of the workshop, painter's techniques and the restorer's contribution

de La Marche, A. Lecoy. *The Manuscripts and the Miniature*. Paris: Maison Quentin, 1884

Gettens, Rutherford J., and Stout, George L. *Painting Materials: A Short Encyclopaedia*. First published, New York: D. Van Nostrand, 1942. Republished by Dover, 1966

Hiler, Hilaire. *The Painter's Pocket Book of Methods and Materials*. London: Faber & Faber, 1937

Lamb, Lynton. *Materials and Methods of Painting*. London: Oxford University Press, 1970

Martin, Dr W. 'How a Dutch Picture was Painted'. London: *The Burlington Magazine*, Vol X (1906), pp 144–54

PATRONAGE, COMMISSIONS, THE ART MARKET

Chamberlain, Betty. *The Artist's Guide to His Market*. New York: Watson-Guptill Publication, 1970. Concentrates on New York galleries and exhibiting

Haskell, Francis. *Patrons and Painters*. London: Chatto & Windus, 1963. A book of great scholarship on the patronage of art in Italy and the relationship between Italian art and society in the age of the Baroque

Lieberman, Alexander. *The Artist in His Studio*. New York: Viking Press, 1960. An intimate book of poetic insight and imagery describing the studio and working life of famous painters of the nineteenth and twentieth centuries.

INDEX

Page numbers in italic type indicate illustrations